A TIME OF CHANGE

A HISTORY OF ENFIELD
Volume Four – 1939 to 1969

A TIME OF CHANGE

BY
Monica Smith

The Enfield Society
2015

ISBN 978-0-907318-23-1

British Library Cataloguing in Publication Data:
A catalogue record for this book is available from the British Library.

Published by The Enfield Society, Jubilee Hall, 2 Parsonage Lane, Enfield EN2 0AJ

Designed by John A. Robey, Ashbourne, DE6 2JR

Printed and bound in Latvia
at Livonia
by arrangement with
Associated Agencies Oxford

Contents

	Acknowledgements	6
	Introduction	7
	Foreword	8
Chapter 1	War	11
Chapter 2	Austerity	37
Chapter 3	The 1950s	51
Chapter 4	The 1960s	70
Chapter 5	Leisure	88
Chapter 6	Transport	106
Chapter 7	Health	122
Chapter 8	Education	136
Chapter 9	Industry & Manufacturing	153
Chapter 10	Enfield Preservation Society	179
Chapter 11	Epilogue — The Changed Scene	203
	Sources & Further Reading	205
	Index	208

Acknowledgements

When the late David Pam told the Enfield Society that he could not undertake the writing of a fourth volume of his successful *History of Enfield*, it was hoped that his successor as Local History Officer for Enfield, Graham Dalling, would agree to do it when he retired, but, sadly, as many readers will know, Graham, died too soon. I was therefore asked to undertake the task, probably because the Management Committee could not think of anyone else. I am not an historian and the resulting book is different from the scholarly research of the first three volumes. It is a social history and the topics covered are influenced by the fact that I lived throughout the period covered and by my own interests and memories.

For much of the information I have relied on previous chroniclers of Enfield, especially Valerie Carter, Graham Dalling, Alan Dumayne, Geoffrey Gillam and David Pam. This has been supplemented by specialist knowledge kindly provided on health by Frank Bayford, on buses by Doug Fairhurst, on Standard Telephone and Cables by Stan Springate, on the British Oxygen Company by Brian Frear and on the Royal Small Arms Factory by Ray Tuthill. My thanks are due to them and also to Jim Lewis and Gordon Hutchinson who used their specialist knowledge to check the chapters titled 'Industry & Manufacturing' and 'Education' respectively.

My other major source was the newspapers, records of meetings, books and pamphlets provided by the Local Studies and Archive of the London Borough of Enfield where John Clark, Kate Godfrey and Annette Sparrowhawk were unfailingly helpful. In addition to the written material they have also provided most of the illustrations from the Borough of Enfield's extensive collection.

Many other photos are from the Enfield Society's own archives and a few from my own collection but I am grateful to those listed below for the loan of the photos and the permission to reproduce them. Despite our research efforts there are a very few of which we have been unable to trace the origin
Enfield Football Club — Graham Frost.
Ferguson's factory — Alexandra Palace Television Group
First cash machine — Barclays Bank
North Middlesex Hospital — Gary Boudier and the North Middlesex University Hospital
Railways — N. L. Cadge and Peter Hill
Historic and listed buildings — Edmonton Camera Club, Enfield Camera Club and Southgate Photographic Society
Cornish Brickworks — Enfield Archaeological Society
School photographs — Enfield County School and the Latymer School

Royal Small Arms Factory — Enfield RSAF Apprentices Association
Buses — Doug Fairhurst,
Princess Margaret at Trent Park — Oliver R. Garrod and Middlesex University
Intimate Theatre — The Geoff Bowden Collection
British Oxygen Company — Edmonton BOC factory
St Paul's School, Winchmore Hill — Peter Hodge
Opening of the above school — St Paul's Archives
Old postcards — Stephen Sellick
Southgate District Civic Trust — SDCT activities and views of Southgate and
    Winchmore Hill
Standard Telephone Company — Stan Springate
Tube trains — The Transport Museum

Several members of the Enfield Society have been very supportive in providing
information and photos but my greatest thanks are to Colin Pointer who not
only edited every draft chapter but also researched and wrote the chapter on
Industry and Manufacturing. I am also grateful to Val Munday and Leonard
Will who played a major role in sourcing appropriate illustrations and prepar-
ing them for reproduction. Finally, on behalf of The Enfield Society I would
like to thank Councillor Michael Rye for agreeing to write the Foreword.

Introduction

This volume is organised differently from the previous three. The first four
chapters are general histories of the war years, the austerity period of the
late 40s, the gradual recovery of the 50s and the prosperous 60s. The other
chapters deal in more detail with the subjects of leisure, transport, health,
education and industry and manufacturing. Chapter 10 summarises the activities of the Enfield Society, then called the Enfield Preservation Society, in
the period. Because the amalgamation of Edmonton, Enfield and Southgate
into the London Borough of Enfield occurred during the years covered by
this volume, I have included information on the three boroughs throughout
the three decades.

Any errors in this book are mine and mine alone.

Monica Smith

Foreword

The period from 1939 to 1969 was indeed a time of major change both nationally and in Enfield. The impact of the Second World War will be familiar to readers from their own family histories, the locality where they live and from wider knowledge. Those who lived through the war; fought or were in reserved occupations, contributed to the home front as Land Army girls, in the many factories (especially the Royal Small Arms Factory at Enfield Lock), as Air Raid Precaution Officers or in many other roles. Everyone from school children to the oldest resident was affected by German raids, national identity cards and this volume evokes, informs and explains the impact of the war on Enfield and the country.

The subsequent period, 'austerity' saw a tired nation having to pay for the war, accept continued rationing and repair to the damage Britain had suffered. At the same time the Government introduced welfare reforms and in 1948 launched the National Health Service. During this period Enfield was served by six hospitals; Highlands, Grovelands, The War Memorial, St Michael`s, Chase Farm and North Middlesex. Everyone had to register at a local doctor's surgery. Despite these changes there were still outbreaks of polio and other diseases. A key requirement in Enfield in 1946 was to build sufficient housing to replace homes lost in the war and for the many returning service personnel. In addition to prefabs, new houses were built by the respective councils which included Enfield's first tower blocks at High View Gardens. Women began to be treated more equally and in 1947 Middlesex County Council followed the lead of the Civil Service by abolishing the ban on the employment of married women.

The 1950s saw a new Government denationalize road transport, increase the wages of the 1.7 million state employees and oversaw average wages double by the end of the decade when compared with 1939. This increased prosperity with many families benefiting from cookers, refrigerators and vacuum cleaners available on deposit and by hire purchase. The first supermarkets opened. Enfield, an Urban District Council, achieved Borough status in 1955 to catch up the Boroughs of Southgate (1933) and Edmonton (1937). In 1957 there was an architectural competition for a new Town Hall at Silver Street, these offices and Council Chamber remain in use today. While some historic buildings were lost to new housing, the UDC of Enfield purchased Forty Hall for £41,000 and was roundly criticized by some for this expenditure!

The 'swinging sixties' brought about the most significant changes to society, with the divorce rate almost doubling, abolition of the death penalty, changed attitudes to homosexuality and abortion and the development of 'popular culture', with greater spending power for young people. In Enfield there were new retail outlets providing the latest fashions and the Education Committee discussed the problem of drugs in schools. Local amenity groups such as Southgate Civic Society and Enfield Preservation Society worked hard with varying success to ensure progress did not remove buildings of historic worth, challenged the council's policies and campaigned to protect the green belt from unwarranted incursions. 1964 saw the creation of the thirty-two London Boroughs, with Edmonton, Enfield and Southgate merging and Potters Bar transferring to Hertfordshire. Various names were discussed for the new borough including Southden and Edengate (interestingly this is perpetuated by a Middlesex Masonic Lodge dedicated to those who give public service in Enfield), before settling upon Enfield. Problems facing the new council remained housing and the need to support older people.

Across the whole period covered by this volume there were other significant changes in transport, education and leisure. The Government was to provide much needed reinvestment in the railways with the lines into Enfield electrified, while trolleybuses were withdrawn and replaced with diesel powered buses. The 1944 Education Act provided free education, separated primary and secondary education with access based upon the Eleven Plus Exam for entry to either a Grammar School or Secondary Modern or Technical School. In Enfield this involved a significant building programme and one of the first new secondary modern schools built was Chase Boys in Churchbury Lane. The biggest change, however, was the new Enfield Borough Council's decision in 1965 to introduce comprehensive education, notwithstanding opposition and protest marches against the change. A compromise saved Latymer Grammar School but with a catchment area of the whole borough.

In leisure the cinema was king with most people going to the cinema at least once a week, at one of many cinemas across the borough like The Plaza in Ponders End, The Alcazar or Regal at Edmonton, Florida or Savoy in Enfield. The introduction and ready availability of televisions from the 1950s would see the number of cinemas in Enfield reduced to just six by 1970. Dancing remained popular while church attendance declined. Sport continued to be popular with participation at many local sports clubs and large attendances were still found at Tottenham and Arsenal football matches, while Enfield FC won the FA Amateur Cup in 1967.

The author has captured the many significant changes of the years 1939-1969, and has written a vibrant local history within the context of what was happening elsewhere cross the British Isles and has risen admirably to the challenge of producing an excellent Volume Four of *A History of Enfield*.

Councillor Michael Rye OBE, London Borough of Enfield

Chapter One

War

I n the final chapter, 'Epilogue: the Approach of War', of his *History of Enfield Volume 3, 1914-39*, David Pam mentioned the measures being put in place in anticipation of war with Germany. Parliament had passed the Air Raid Precautions Act (ARP) and Edmonton, Enfield and Southgate Councils had started to make preparations for war. Edmonton Council published a leaflet explaining that 'A warning will be sounded when an air attack is expected. It consists of a wailing sound on a variable pitch. When

1   Digging trenches on Library Green

2   *The Fire Service tug-of-war team*

3   *Women and children carrying gasmasks*

4   An air-raid shelter, Gordon Hill

5   Anderson shelters in Cuckoo Hall Lane

6   *High explosive bombs destroyed the Anderson shelters in Chapel Street, Enfield*

the air raid has passed there will be a blast on one note to signify all clear'. All three councils appointed a full time ARP Officer and appeals were made for volunteer air raid wardens, ambulance drivers and auxiliary firemen. Response at first was very slow, especially when Chamberlain's 'Peace in Our Time' appeasement agreement in September 1938 gave hope that war was not inevitable, but increased from March 1939 when Germany invaded and annexed Czechoslovakia. Enfield planned to have sixty-seven ARP posts and by the outbreak of war on 3 September 1939, 2,800 local men and women had agreed to undertake ARP duties. By the end of the war 30,000 people were engaged in civil defence and auxiliary services in Enfield.

Volunteers were needed to supplement the small number of regular members of the Fire Brigade. In the first issue of *Fireworks*, the magazine of the Southgate AFS (Auxiliary Fire Service), the Chief Fire Officer wrote: 'In 1938 on the instructions of the Home Office, personnel for the auxiliary fire service were sought in Southgate. I was amazed at the response and enthusiasm by which the appeal was answered'. Southgate's regular unit consisted of only four officers and nineteen firemen and this was increased by forty-eight auxiliaries. Other preparations included rehearsals of the sirens which would warn of the approach of enemy aircraft, the issue of gas masks to all residents and the conversion of the trenches, dug earlier in parks and open spaces, into communal air raid shelters by lining and roofing them with concrete. Thousands of Anderson shelters were delivered to homes and were free of charge to those with an annual income below £350. Back gardens were dug up

7   *Grovelands House was used a casualty hospital*

to bury them half in the ground with earth on top. By October 1939 Enfield had provided 4,719 of these shelters but the shortage of steel stopped their manufacture until April 1940. Once the air raids began many families slept in theirs every night. Unfortunately they did not guarantee complete protection and some were seriously damaged by high explosive bombs. Shelters were also built at some schools and shops, such as the department store, Evans and Davies, Palmers Green. Plans for the evacuation of children and mothers with babies from London and other large cities were drawn up.

Enfield's hospital services had been augmented shortly before the outbreak of war by the opening of Chase Farm, a large general hospital which, together with the North Middlesex, Highlands and Grovelands, were now adapted to treat the casualties of air raids. When war was declared it was realised that additional facilities would be needed and supplementary first aid and ambulance stations were set up in places such as Barrowell Green Swimming Baths, Broomfield House, Houndsfield School and Pymmes House. All places of entertainment were closed although some cinemas and the Intimate Theatre re-opened within a month, The three year old BBC television service was cancelled and broadcasts on the radio were, like the newspapers, subject to censorship so that they gave no information which might be of value to the enemy. The radio assumed great importance during the war years. Most families listened to the Nine O'Clock News for an update on the war situation and there were morale-boosting speeches by the Prime Minister, Winston Churchill. It is estimated that 70 per cent of the population listened to his

8   *Pymmes House was used an emergency first-aid station until destroyed by fire in 1940*

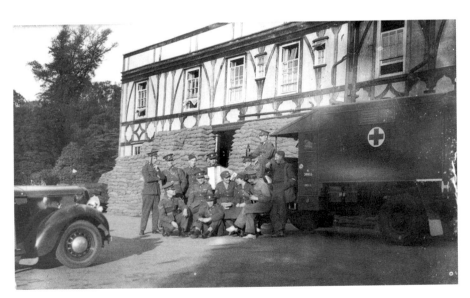

9. Volunteers at Broomfield House

broadcasts, which were sometimes repeats of what he had said in the House of Commons. Other broadcasters such as the Radio Doctor offered advice on health and diet. There were also comedy and children's programmes to entertain listeners while 'Music While You Work' was broadcast to factories to spur the workers on to greater efficiency.

10   Sandbag protection was provided for key buildings

The street scene changed as all windows had to be blacked out after dark and those whose premises showed a light were prosecuted and their appearance in court was reported in the local papers. Sandbags protected the entrances of key buildings such as police stations and outside many front doors buckets of water and sand were seen which the *Gazette* of 1 September 1939 had urged householders to prepare 'for use in case of fire'. Barrage balloons were a common sight; flying several hundred feet above parks and open spaces where they were tethered, their purpose was to prevent enemy aircraft flying low. There were anti-aircraft batteries in places such as Firs Farm Playing Fields, in a field north of Slades Hill and in Enfield Playing Fields. The recent obituary of Lady Soames, the youngest daughter of Sir Winston Churchill, mentioned that she joined the ATS (Auxiliary Territorial Service) in 1941 and served at one of the anti-aircraft sites in Enfield.

On 22 September 1939 petrol was the first item to be rationed and only those for whose war work a vehicle was considered essential were issued with coupons. As a result most family cars were put on blocks for six years. Misuse of the petrol allocation could result in a fine or imprisonment as one Enfield secretary found out when she used her car to drive to a public house for lunch. Travel became very difficult and was discouraged so 'holidays at home' replaced weeks at the seaside. The beaches, in any case, had been made inaccessible by barbed wire barriers and some were mined.

The destruction of places such as Guernica by the Luftwaffe (the German

11   *An anti-aircraft battery on Slades Hill*

12   *Edmonton pupils were evacuated initially to Clacton*

13   Land Army girls working on a local farm

14   Land Army girls farming in Oakwood Park

Air Force) during the Spanish Civil War, which had ended as recently as April 1939, was remembered by many who feared that British towns too would be attacked by aerial bombardment. The evacuation of children was not compulsory but was offered in 1939 to all families living in industrialised

Edmonton and eastern Enfield but not to those in Southgate and The Town and western areas of Enfield which were considered to be less at risk. Edmonton children were sent mostly to Essex; pupils from Edmonton County School went to Braintree, Latymer students to Clacton and those from Eldon School to Silver End near Witham. When the expected bombing of London did not happen, many children returned home in early 1940, although some went back to the country later that year when London was attacked in the Blitz. Foster parents were paid 10s 6d (52p) per week for one evacuee staying with them and 17s (85p) for two. Parents contributed according to their income.

Some local men and women had volunteered to join the Army, Navy or Air Force in 1939 and compulsory conscription for all men between twenty and forty-one was enforced in 1941. Those who refused to serve in the armed forces were called conscientious objectors and were required to submit their reasons. Each case was heard by a military tribunal and, if excused, they were issued with a Certificate of Registration on the Register of Conscientious Objectors. Conscription for women followed in 1942 and many undertook jobs which had previously been a male preserve such as postmen and railway porters. Others joined the Land Army and provided agricultural labour on farms including some of those in the local green belt and parks. Most, however, replaced men in the arms factories. Government day nurseries were set up to care for the small children of working mothers.

In 1940, following the fall of France and the retreat from Dunkirk, a German invasion of Britain was feared. Everyone was issued with Identity Cards which they had to carry at all times and show if challenged. Defences were built to

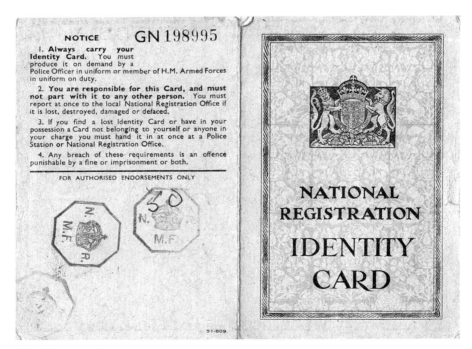

15   *Identity card*

16   The 30ᵗʰ Battalion of the Middlesex Home Guard on parade in 1943

hinder any invading forces. These included pill boxes and anti-tank blocks in
such places as Ponders End Station, the Rose & Crown in Clay Hill and the
junction of Hedge Lane and Hoppers Road. All signposts, names on railway
stations and other signs which could identify the locality were removed to
confuse invaders. It was also decided to supplement the army by a force of
volunteers called at first Local Defence Volunteers and later the Home Guard.
Subsequently, it was dubbed 'Dad's Army' and was immortalised in the long
running comedy television series. There were six battalions in our area and
the units were manned initially by World War 1 veterans, those too old, too
young (under eighteen) or unfit for military service and some men who were
in reserved occupations, for example at the Royal Small Arms Factory, because
of their special skills. Many of the units were workplace based, including the
56th Essex Home Guard which was formed of RSAF volunteers. The Home
Guard's first tasks were to protect telephone exchanges, post offices, water,
gas, electric and other essential services but with the arrival of the Blitz in 1940
they assisted the ARP wardens in rescuing victims of the bombing and shoring
up dangerous buildings. Later they also manned some of the anti-aircraft
guns and controlled road junctions. The ARP wardens were also helped by
members of the Women's Voluntary Service (WVS). Many women had been
anxious to contribute to the war effort and 600,000 throughout Britain
joined this organisation and there were branches in Edmonton, Enfield and

17 (above)   An ARP
warden's post

18 (right)   An ARP
telephone box

Southgate. They helped with first aid, provided tea, meals and temporary accommodation for those who had lost their homes. They also assisted the organisation of salvage campaigns for metal and paper, which today we would call recycling, and acted as messengers. Other volunteers, equipped with stirrup pumps, regularly spent the night on the roofs of office, factory and other large buildings to deal with fires caused by incendiary bombs which were expected, and did fall in great numbers.

There were some regular forces stationed in the area. A detachment from a Tank Repair Unit was billeted in Bycullah Road and established their workshop and repair yard in the car park of the Savoy Cinema, Southbury Road. Naval personnel were based at *HMS Cockfosters*, a building in Hadley Wood where they were trained in the operation of port facilities, which was to be especially crucial for the D-Day invasion of Europe by allied forces.

19 (above)   Civil Defence volunteers demonstrate the use of stirrup pumps

MINISTRY OF FOOD

RATION BOOK

JULY 1943 ISSUE

Surname....*HELLIAR*

Other Names....*BETTY L*

Address....*29 Beechdale N 21*
(as on Identity Card)

IF UNDER 18 YEARS

State date of birth (Day)....(Month)....(Year)....

NATIONAL REGISTRATION NUMBER *DFKF 132 4*   R.B.1 GENERAL

IF FOUND RETURN TO

L73 LONDON

FOOD OFFICE

Z 590389

20 (right)   Ration book

One consequence of the German occupation of France, Belgium and the Netherlands was the arrival of refugees — the first recorded group consisted of eighty people with an age range of seven weeks to eighty years from the Brussels and Ostend areas of Belgium. Obituaries of the first local servicemen killed in action appeared in the local papers and these were to continue throughout the war.

21   A queue for fish

22 Dig for Victory campaign

23   Bush Hill Park was converted
into allotments

   In 1940 food rationing was introduced for a few items including meat,
tea and cooking fat. Ration books were distributed to all and weekly
limits were set at 1s 3d worth of meat (about 6p in today's currency), 8oz
of fat, 2oz tea.   In 1941 rationing was extended to jam, cheese, eggs and
milk. Children had an increased ration of milk and there was free milk for
schoolchildren. Babies had a special allocation of items such as cod liver oil
and orange juice. New goods such as powdered egg and dried skimmed milk
supplemented the basic ration and from 1943 whale meat was available at
some butchers but was never popular. Oranges, bananas, ice cream and white
bread disappeared from the shops. The number of food items rationed was
increased still further in 1942 when rice, dried fruits, tinned tomatoes and
peas and biscuits were added. The main purpose of rationing was to ensure
an even distribution of limited produce and prevent a black market but one
did exist, especially for scarce food items, petrol and cigarettes and many
prosecutions which resulted are reported from the local courts. The seas
around Britain were mined by the German navy and patrolled by German
submarines called U-boats. It was therefore difficult and dangerous for the
Merchant Navy to ship food to Britain and fishing vessels could not go to sea.
Cargo vessels were destroyed and many seamen lost their lives. Fish was not
rationed but was very scarce and there were long queues to buy what little was
available. A 'Dig for Victory' campaign was established to encourage more
home produced food. In the market gardens of the Lea Valley edible crops
replaced flowers, and tomatoes were grown instead of cucumbers as the latter
were considered to have little nutritional value. Enfield farmers planted an
additional 200 acres with food crops and there were Land Girls working at
Forty Hill Farm. Allotments were in great demand and 1,000 additional ones
were provided in Edmonton alone, and many more in parks and open spaces
of Enfield and Southgate. Residents also grew vegetables instead of flowers
in their gardens and some kept chickens and rabbits to supplement the meat
ration. Housewives bottled surplus summer fruit and vegetables in Kilner
jars to preserve them for winter meals. The campaign was so successful that
by 1945 Britain was importing only a third of its food requirements. The
recycling of food was encouraged then as now. Swill bins appeared on many
streets: vegetable and fruit peelings, meat bones and uneaten food would
be placed in them to be boiled up and fed to pigs. Some businesses dealt in
goods strange to them. Winchmore Hill Garage, which would have had little
petrol to sell because of rationing, became a meat depot when Smithfield

24. Damage at Willow Road caused by a landmine

25   The bomb at Ponders End wrecked a public house and two schools

*26   In March 1941 three bombs destroyed a dance hall, a bank and a bus in Green Lanes,
Palmers Green*

Market in central London was considered a likely target for bombs and meat
distribution was dispersed to smaller units.

In 1942 a law was passed by which restaurants were not allowed to charge
more than 5s (25p) for a meal. A cheap plain standard meal could be obtained
in one of the British Restaurants which were set up throughout London. The
first one in Enfield was opened in October 1941 in Eastfield Road. Some
schoolchildren who had not been evacuated walked daily to one in a Palmers
Green cinema for lunch. There was a scandal in 1941 when Southgate's
Catering Officer, who was in charge of this and other restaurants, was found to
have been making purchases from irregular sources and some dishes on the
menu were found to include horsemeat instead of beef. He was successfully
prosecuted for this offence and also, somewhat bizarrely, for having in his
possession 'a large quantity of custard powder'. Recipes from the Ministry
of Food for wartime meals using the limited ingredients available appeared
every week in the local press, including one 'How to make carrot jam without
sugar'.

In 1940 the so-called phoney war ended and the Luftwaffe started to attack
Britain, targeting especially RAF bases and aircraft factories. In July the Battle
of Britain began. In August a force of German bombers was intercepted over
the Enfield/Edmonton border by a squadron of RAF fighters. One German

plane was shot down over Ponders End Sewage Works and another crashed into glasshouses in Durants Road. Many people thronged the streets to witness the fight. On 7 September the target was the London Docks and the resulting fires were so huge they could be seen from our area. On 14 November a further bombardment of London began and the City and the West End bore the brunt of the prolonged attack with severe damage to buildings and loss of life. Regular and auxiliary firemen from all the outer London boroughs were sent to assist the local fire brigades in the East End, City and West End and many worked for twenty-four hours without a break.

Because so many had been made homeless by these raids local authorities were given the power to requisition private property. In Enfield and Southgate many houses were under construction at the outbreak of war and therefore unsold and families, particularly those from the East End, were re-housed in them. The Enfield area had suffered much less than the central zone but three landmines caused damage and loss of life. One at the junction of Willow and Peartree Roads flattened a row of houses and killed four members of a family. The second landed in London Road and destroyed the Roman Catholic Church and some houses and the third caused extensive damage to the Royal Small Arms Factory and broke thousands of panes of glass in nearby greenhouses. A special licence was allowed to the growers to acquire glass, an item which was in short supply and not available to replace household windows. The repair of this damage was considered essential to the production of food. A bomb fell at the junction of South Street and Ponders End High Road, wrecking the Two Brewers public house and damaging two churches, the Congregational and St Matthews. The Alcazar Cinema in Fore Street, Edmonton was destroyed. In October the pipelines carrying the water of the New River from Southbury Road were shattered by a bomb and parts of Bush Hill Park were flooded. Two thousand soldiers of the Pioneer Corps dug out the filled in section of the original course and the water flowed once more through the Enfield Loop until the pipes were replaced. The worst local incident occurred in March 1941 when a string of bombs fell in Green Lanes, Palmers Green: one landed outside the crowded Princes Dance Hall where a queue of people at the bus stop and the passengers and crew of a bus bore the full force of the explosion. Sixty-nine people died and many others suffered dreadful injuries from flying glass.

Homes which did not have Anderson shelters were in 1940 offered Morrison shelters. Basically these were large metal tables placed inside the house under which several people could sleep. However many homes were still without any shelter and a quarter of a million Londoners sought refuge every night by sleeping on the platforms of London Underground stations. All the local stations were, however, unsuitable as Arnos Grove, Oakwood (then called Enfield West) and Cockfosters stations are above ground and Southgate has a short tunnel to the outside. There was a serious incident just outside the borough boundary at Bounds Green when a bomb caused the tunnel to collapse killing people who were sleeping on the platforms, including some Belgian refugees.

On 7 December 1941 the Japanese Air Force bombed Pearl Harbour and this led to the United States declaring war on both Germany and Japan. Thousands of American troops began to arrive in Britain together with planes and equipment. Britain had fought alone for two years but now she had a powerful ally.

27 (right)   *A book of clothing coupons*

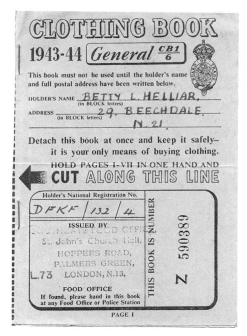

28 (below)   *Trent Park was used as an interrogation centre and prison for enemy officers*

In 1942 clothes rationing was brought in. Everyone had an allocation of points and each item had a points value so choices had to be made about which items to buy. This presented especial problems for families with growing children and schools organised the sale of second hand uniforms. There were many 'hand me downs' between family and friends. 'Make Do and Mend' was another campaign slogan and clothes were repaired and re-fashioned. A girl's green school blazer was dyed black, the buttons and buttonholes reversed, and the badge changed for a younger male member of the family. Soap was added to the list of items rationed and then sweets and chocolate. Public houses remained open but beer was often in short supply while wine and other imported drinks were almost unobtainable. In 1942 there was a scrap metal drive and iron gates and railings were removed from hundreds of houses, allegedly to be used for armaments, although there have since been doubts that the metal was suitable for this purpose and that it was, in fact, dumped in the North Sea.

Trent Park mansion was one of three stately homes converted into interrogation centres for high ranking German and Italian prisoners, captured mostly during the North Africa campaign of 1942. A recent book by Helen Fry and a television documentary 'Spying on Hitler's Army' broadcast in June 2013 on Channel 4, describe the role played by a team of German and Austrian refugees who had come to Britain in the 1930s. They were given the task of listening to the prisoners' private conversations, which included reminiscences and confessions, and recording anything of interest which was then translated into English. Microphones were hidden in cells and other rooms and even the trees in Trent Park were bugged. Details of German armaments and equipment and news of the German surrender and defeat at Stalingrad were gleaned in this way. It was also an early source of awareness of the existence

29. Chesterfield Road School was hit by a V1 rocket in 1944

30   *Damage caused by a V2 at Pevensey Avenue, New Southgate*

and atrocities of the concentration camps such as Auschwitz and the German Army's involvement in the Holocaust. Hearing this latter information must have been especially difficult for the listeners who were mostly Jewish. The biggest coup was the advance information on rocket warfare as the RAF were then able to bomb the rocket production site and delay the V2 attacks on Britain. The prisoners were given a false sense of security and spoke to one another in what they thought was privacy. The recordings were destroyed but 49,000 transcripts have now come to light. Prisoners of lower ranks were housed in large POW camps built between Bullsmoor Lane and the Great Cambridge Road and at the northern end of the King George Playing Fields.

After May 1941 enemy action over London was intermittent until 1944 when there was a series of hit and run raids. In one of these a bomb fell on Bell Lane, Enfield Highway and another on the North Middlesex Hospital in Edmonton where several people were killed. This is thought to be one of the last bombs to fall on Britain from a piloted aircraft. Then in 1944 the V1 unmanned flying bombs, known as doodle bugs, began to fall. There was a three minute siren warning when they would be heard approaching and people soon learned to seek cover when the engine cut out as the bomb was about to fall to earth and explode. One landed near Ordnance Road, destroying part of Chesterfield Road School and St Peter and St Paul Church. Another direct hit was on the factory of United Flexible Tubing in Scotland Green Road. A public house was wrecked in Fore Street, Edmonton near the junction with Fairfield Road and several houses were destroyed with

31. *Mapleton Road, Enfield Highway after an attack by a V2*

32. *Clearing up after a V2 incident in Abbey Road, Bush Hill Park*

much loss of life in Carpenter Gardens, Winchmore Hill. In total thirty-five V1s fell locally: seven in Edmonton, twenty-two in Enfield and six in Southgate.

The V1 attack was followed by the V2 rockets which travelled faster than sound, gave no warning of their approach and did massive damage. One fell at Mapleton Road, Enfield Highway in March and another in Bush Hill Park in December 1944, destroying houses and killing and injuring many people. Other V2s fell at the junction of Gordon and Lavender Hills, and in New Southgate. One exploded on the railway track between Palmers Green Station and Fox Lane Bridge. There was a train in the station at the time and a passenger was killed by debris falling through the carriage roof. The gasworks in Angel Road were badly damaged. Houses, shops and offices which were not destroyed or badly damaged often had their windows blown out by the blast. The windows were replaced with board as glass was not available so that the premises could continue to be occupied. Large windows in shops were often covered in Splinternet, a specially tested adhesive fabric stuck on the glass to prevent it shattering into dangerous splinters.

Industries of the area played an important part in the supply to the armed forces of ammunition and equipment including guns, shells, rifles, anti-submarine devices, radar, civil defence equipment and landing barges. Edmonton's furniture factories made parts for the Mosquito bomber, one of the outstanding aircraft of the war. It was built almost entirely of wood which had the benefit of rendering it almost invisible to German radar. The Metal Box factory made parts for gas masks and British Oxygen was involved in a project to use ether for cold starting petrol and diesel engines on the Russian front but the system was only perfected as the war ended. For more details of Enfield's industry and its war time contribution see Chapter 9 'Industry and Manufacturing'.

With the D-Day invasion of Europe and the gradual retreat and defeat of the German army in 1944, victory seemed to be in sight and there was no threat of an invasion, so in 1945 the Civil Defence held stand-down parades. The three local councils began to consider plans for the post war development of their boroughs and the considerable challenges they faced. The total damage was estimated at 433 houses destroyed in Edmonton, 347 in Enfield and 256 in Southgate. Fatalities were similarly highest in Edmonton with 162, Enfield 109 and Southgate 118 deaths.

War in Europe ended on 8 May 1945 with the surrender of Germany and the death of Hitler. Churches were filled to capacity for thanksgiving services and there were parties and dancing in the streets and the parks. Church bells rang out for the first time in nearly six years – during the war the ringing would have signalled Britain had been invaded. British prisoners of war from European camps began to return home. Japan surrendered in August 1945 following the dropping of atomic bombs on Hiroshima and Nagasaki. Local councils organised celebrations with bonfires and a victory beacon in Broomfield Park and a service and celebration in Pymmes Park, Edmonton. Parties were held in many streets of the three boroughs. Later in the year, the survivors of the Japanese camps came home. Some German and Italian prisoners were returned to their countries but a few of the Italians remained in the Lea Valley to work in the market gardens and local papers record that some 300 German prisoners were still living in the POW camps at Christmas

*33   Celebrating
Victory in Europe
— May 1945*

34   VJ (Victory over Japan) celebrations in Pymmes Park, August 1945

35   One of many street parties held to celebrate the end of the war.

1946 and were employed in manual work including laying the sewers at Reservoir Road,

Churchill resigned as Prime Minister on 23 May 1945 but formed a caretaker government to run the country until a general election could be held. This took place in July 1945 with a landslide victory for the Labour Party by 393 seats to the Conservatives' 213. In Enfield Ernest Davies won the seat for Labour while Beverley Baxter (Conservative) continued as MP for Southgate and Wood Green. The successful Labour candidate in Edmonton, Evan Durbin, was regarded as a high flyer who had been on Mr Attlee's staff during the war, but tragically he was drowned three years later. Mr Attlee became Prime Minister and announced his programme was 'to implement social security reform and to start the National Health Service'. The Beveridge Report had been published in December 1942 by the wartime Coalition Government and had the support of some Conservative members, such as Anthony Eden and Harold Macmillan, as well as Labour MPs. It was a blueprint for a welfare state, concerned with social insurance and full employment but implementation had clearly been impossible during the war. Its mantra was 'Freedom from want by securing to each a minimum income sufficient for subsistence'.

The war had been long and costly to Britain — an estimate is £700 million. The country was heavily in debt. Many things had to change and tough times lay ahead.

CHAPTER 2
Austerity

The euphoria produced by the relief that the war was over and a certain pride in Britain's role in the victory did not last long. Post-war Britain was an austere place. The cost of the long war had left it heavily in debt and the Lend Lease agreement, by which the US Government had given the countries fighting Germany and Japan whatever they needed, was abruptly ended by President Truman eight days after the ceasefire. Britain's debt for this loan was $30 million. In 1947 it was replaced by Marshall Aid which the American Government offered to European countries to help them rebuild their economies. In the view of the editor of the *Palmers Green & Southgate Gazette* 'but for Marshall Aid Britain would have collapsed'. However this loan of $3.5 million came with costly strings attached. The USA required Britain to bear a share of the costs and responsibilities of the resistance to the communist threat. In addition to the financial costs it would result in British regular and national service troops serving in Germany, Greece, Aden, Malaya and the Middle East. From 1946 news of the crushing of European democracies by Stalinism was prominent in the newspapers and marked the start of what George Orwell named 'The Cold War'. In that year, Winston Churchill, on a visit to the United States at the invitation of President Truman, said 'An iron curtain has descended over Europe' — he was the first western statesman to single out communism as an enemy.

After the end of the war food rationing not only continued but some allocations were actually reduced as the pressure on the limited supplies increased. Food had to be sent to several countries, including Germany, in mainland Europe where people were dying of starvation because most of the agricultural industries had been destroyed by the war. A Famine Relief Committee was set up and meetings were organised locally including one at Bowes Park Methodist Church which had 'Save Europe from Starvation' as its theme. Wheat especially was in such short supply that for the first time bread was rationed. 'A normal adult' was given nine bread points per week which would purchase three large loaves or two loaves and half a pound of flour. There were larger entitlements for pregnant women, adolescents and manual workers. In July 1946 Enfield bakers organised a protest against bread rationing but it achieved no change. A sign of things to come was an advertisement by Tesco in the *Tottenham and Edmonton Herald* of March 1946 with the slogan 'You can see what you are buying at a Tesco store'. The supermarkets were coming but most people continued to buy food at their local shops with which

36 *Many servicemen married in the 1940s*

they were registered for their rations of meat and groceries. The Ministry of Food continued its wartime practice of publishing 'helpful hints' in local papers: for example, 'How to make scones without fat' and 'Tasty meals from corned beef'; a small amount of the latter had been added to the meat ration. What was new was the continual stress on not wasting bread. Two groups of residents escaped the shortages and austerity. Girls, who had married American or Canadian servicemen posted to Britain, were now able to join their husbands in North America and the local newspapers showed photos of some of them and their children on departure. Other families decided to emigrate to New Zealand, Canada and especially to Australia which offered subsidised travel to many.

A big problem was housing, because not only had over 1,000 houses been completely destroyed in Edmonton, Enfield and Southgate, but almost every dwelling needed attention because no painting or maintenance had been carried out for over five years. Thousands of broken window panes were gradually replaced. An advertisement of January 1946 by the local electrical supply company, Northmet, informed their customers that 'most of the glass had been replaced in their showrooms'.

The acute shortage of accommodation was increased by the return to civilian life of 750,000 service personnel. In Enfield alone the Food Office in January 1946 was dealing with requests for ration books from 150 ex-servicemen and women every day. There were a great many weddings of couples who had been separated by the war and this led to a rapid rise in the birth rate and, consequently, even more over-crowding. Pre-fabricated bungalows, known as 'prefabs' offered a partial solution in Enfield and Edmonton but Southgate decided to build only permanent homes. The prefabs, built in former aircraft factories, were not cheap as they cost £550 each but they could be assembled

37.   Prefabricated bungalows in Delhi Road

38   Re-building of Cuckoo Hall Estate

*39 (above) New
council housing,
Barrowell Green*

*40 (left) Slum
clearance at Gilpin
Crescent*

41   *Opening of the Harlow New Town exhibition. Evan Durbin MP, second from the left*

quickly and the first ones were ready for occupation by January 1946. The families who moved into them are reported as finding them 'comfortable and pleasant'. Enfield Urban District Council rehoused 1,019 families in 1946, either in these or in requisitioned buildings. The first new permanent housing in Enfield in November 1946 was built on the site of the bomb which fell at Enfield Highway. Southgate's first new dwellings were in Barrowell Green while Edmonton's housing drive began with the building of a large number of homes on the Cuckoo Hall Estate. Another way of easing the housing crisis was for people to be encouraged to move to the New Towns such as Harlow and Stevenage. Edmonton had the most acute housing problem as it had suffered most from the bombing, had large areas of slums which needed clearing or modernising and little land for development. Edmonton had links with Harlow New Town through one of its councillors, Tom Joyce, who was vice-chairman of the Harlow Development Corporation. An exhibition was held in Edmonton Town Hall and in 1948 local people began to move to Harlow. Later Edmonton also built estates in Cheshunt and Potters Bar. According to reports in the *Herald*, there were 'mixed feelings' about life in the New Towns. Southgate decided not to build outside the borough boundaries. Most housing in Old Southgate was not in a bad condition so in 1956 Southgate Council concentrated on the redevelopment of parts of New Southgate with the first tower blocks in the district. Neither Enfield nor Southgate could expand to the north because of the green belt legislation. In some areas, such as the Bycullah Estate, large houses began to be divided into four or five flats, a trend which has continued.

Despite the ending of hostilities in August 1945 obituaries continued in

42 The first tower blocks, High View Gardens

the local newspapers of men and women who had been reported missing but whose death could not be confirmed until the war ended. National Service of two years in one of the armed services, mostly the army, continued for all men over eighteen, many of whom served in conflicts overseas such as Palestine, Greece and Aden. National Service was abolished for women.

There were stand-down parades for the Civil Defence units and the Home Guard but the Women's Voluntary Service (WVS) continued to operate in new directions such as Meals on Wheels for the housebound . In December 1946 it organised a one-off distribution to twenty schools of ten tons of chocolate milk powder which had been donated by Canada to the children of Britain.

In June 1946 Victory Parades were held both nationally and locally. Each of the three councils organised similar celebrations with processions, (Edmonton's was led by the Mayor on horseback), which included ex-servicemen and women and representatives of the Fire Service, St John's Ambulance, Red Cross, ARP, Home Guard and other civilian organisations which had played a vital role on the home front. There were also sports for children, dancing in the parks, fireworks, music recitals and concert party entertainments.

In 1945 the Labour Government won the general election and it was thought that the desire for change was a key factor in their landslide success. In 1946 they introduced one of the first welfare reforms when families were paid a weekly allowance for every child except the first. The National Health Service followed in 1948 and the nationalisation began of 20 per cent of the economy, including coal, steel, railways, airlines, the Bank of England, gas and electricity. It was assumed that public ownership of these key industries would lead to greater productivity and a financial gain for the public purse rather than for private investors. Another change locally was that Enfield Urban District Council decided to follow Edmonton's practice and operate

43   *Victory Parade, 1946, Enfield*

a 'closed shop' policy which made it a condition of employment that all their employees should be members of the appropriate union.

The Representation of the People Act set up a Boundary Commission to review electoral boundaries with the result that by the time of the 1950 general election there would be separate constituencies for Wood Green and Southgate and East and West ones in Enfield.

1947 has become known as the most difficult year. It was a bitterly cold winter with seven weeks of temperatures below freezing so that domestic pipes and tanks froze and many families were left without water. Coal was in short supply and deliveries were hampered by roads blocked by snowdrifts. Households were asked to economise on the use of electricity so that the factories could continue production but in January several factories in Enfield and Edmonton had to close and 14,000 workers were laid off. The weather and a strike at Smithfield Meat Market affected the supply of fresh food and for the first time potatoes became scarce. In January lorries, driven by soldiers from the Coldstream Guards, brought the first supply of fresh meat to Enfield for three weeks, as a result of the strike and the transport problems; it was distributed to sixty-three butchers' shops. The young enjoyed skating in Pymmes Park and on other lakes and tobogganing at Hilly Fields but for most people it was an exceedingly cold, difficult and miserable time.

The summer was however gloriously sunny and half the population had their first holiday for eight years. During the heat wave a temperature of 95°F (35°C) was recorded in Fore Street, Edmonton. Seaside resorts such as Margate and Clacton and the re-opened Butlin's Holiday Camps were popular destinations. Travel abroad was difficult because so many countries in mainland Europe had to rebuild their hotels and their infrastructure after the devastation of the war but an estimated 3 per cent went to places such as Switzerland. Because of the economic situation the amount of foreign currency each traveller was allowed was small and strictly controlled and had

44   Tobogganing at Hilly Fields

45   Islington Cemetery, Trent Park

to cover all costs of accommodation, entertainment and meals while abroad.

The prisoners of war detained in Trent Park had been repatriated and a temporary teacher training college was set up in the mansion to assist with the staff shortages in schools. Trent Park was also in the news when many Southgate residents expressed their opposition to the Borough of Islington's application to develop 120 acres of the green belt on the Trent Park Estate as a cemetery. However in August Islington Council was granted a compulsory purchase order and construction of the cemetery went ahead.

Soon after he became Prime Minister Mr Attlee had resumed the talks on Indian independence which had begun before the war. The sub-continent was divided into two independent nations, India and Pakistan in August 1947 and the dissolution of the Empire began.

The Royal Wedding in November 1947 briefly lightened the gloom as London saw the return of some colour and pageantry. All the local papers printed photographs and sent greetings and good wishes to the Princess Elizabeth and Lieutenant Philip Mountbatten on their marriage. One fifteen-year-old scout from Southgate was selected as an usher at the Westminster Abbey service.

For women World War II acted as a catalyst for change, much as World War I had for their mothers. In 1947 Middlesex County Council followed the example of the Civil Service and abolished the ban on the employment of married women. Before 1939 a third of working women were in service as maids, nannies, cooks or waitresses but during the war they had been drafted into factories, worked in offices and on railways, buses and tubes and undertaken, successfully, other jobs which had previously been a male preserve. Most had no wish or intention to return to domestic work. One consequence of this was an increased demand for vacuum cleaners, washing machines, refrigerators and other electrical appliances which were available in the late 1940s as many housewives began to do their own housework for the first time. Women began to yearn for a change of clothes from the dowdy, practical ones they had worn during the war. 1947 was the year that Christian Dior opened his Paris fashion house with the 'New Look', a return to glamorous dresses with billowing skirts. Advertisments for such clothes appeared in the local papers and Pearsons advised readers that they now had 'negligees and lingerie on sale.' Trousers for women, called slacks, had been practical during the war for working in factories, sleeping in air raid shelters or underground stations and some women continued to wear them at times. This did not please the Vicar of St Mary the Virgin Church, Edmonton who condemned the wearing of trousers and make-up in church by women as 'unsuitable'.

Although the devaluation of the pound made all imported goods more costly, 1948 was an improvement on the previous year. There were many job vacancies, including for women in factories such as Edison Swan and in government offices where a shorthand typist's salary was £5 a week. The transport systems also regularly advertised vacancies for drivers and conductors.

A by-election was held in Edmonton because of the tragic death of the talented and popular MP, Evan Durbin, who drowned while trying to rescue a child in Cornwall. The seat was held for Labour with a much reduced majority by Austen Albu. The unpopularity of the Attlee Government and the Palestine situation were thought to have been responsible for the decline in support for the Labour candidate. Mr Albu, however, continued to represent Edmonton in Parliament for many more years. British soldiers had been killed in Palestine by Jewish terrorists and this had resulted in anti-Semitism in Edmonton, and Mr Albu was Jewish.

The Olympic Games were held in London in the summer of 1948. They have become known as 'The Austerity Games' because competitors were asked to bring their own food. Despite taking place in a war-scarred city with athletes accommodated in old army camps, the Games were considered a triumph. Two members of Southgate Harriers were selected to be part of the British team: S. Cox in the 10,000 metres and J. Giles in 'putting the weight'. From Enfield, P. Valle ran in the 200 metres and J. Rawlings was a member of the football team. Three local officials also took part.

The British Nationality Act of 1948 which was passed by Parliament was to have an effect on the decade ahead. All 800 million subjects of the king were to be regarded as British citizens with the right to live in the United Kingdom. It was assumed that Asians and Africans would not wish to move to the United Kingdom, especially since travel then was very expensive. Nearly all the thousands of Caribbean, Indian and other soldiers from the Empire and the Dominions who had served with British forces during the war had returned home in 1945.

People had more money to spend as wages had increased significantly, partly as a result of the heavy demand from Europe for the electrical goods produced locally but also because of pressure from the unions. Most people began to enjoy holidays and day trips by coach, train and *Eagle* steamer to the sea and places of interest.. However, there were new problems. In its summary of 1948 the *Enfield Gazette* highlighted the increase in vandalism with the

46   Austen Albu's by-election poster

headline 'Hooliganism rampant in Enfield — public and private property damaged'.

By 1949 things were looking up. The allocation of some rations such as tea was increased, certain items were no longer rationed, the soap allowance was doubled and, to the delight of children, sweet rationing ended. More imported items were seen in the shops. One advert encouraged shoppers to buy new clothes with 'Practically all suits, jackets and trousers are coupon free' and during that year clothing coupons were abolished. Clothes under the Utility label were still on sale: they were all that there had been available to buy for many years and had been deliberately designed to save material with fewer pockets and no turn-ups on trousers. Utility furniture too had been plain and functional but now modern designs in fabrics, crockery and furniture were in the shops, some of them made from the surplus of material no longer needed for war planes or landing craft. So Perspex intended for gun turrets on bombers was used for table tops, while sofas and armchairs were upholstered in RAF uniform cloth. New cars were on sale and as traffic increased on the roads so did the number of accidents, especially to pedestrians and cyclists. As a consequence of this the government introduced a new campaign, 'Keep Death off the Roads.'

For women there was welcome news when Mrs Jay became the first female Chairman of Enfield Urban District Council and in July 1949 female employees of the UDC celebrated as, for the first time, they were allowed to join their male colleagues on the annual staff outing to Southend.

The war had softened class differences as people had united in one effort to win the war: public schoolboys had found themselves working in coal mines

47 (left)   Mrs Jay, the first woman chairman of Enfield UDC

48 (Below)   Enfield Town in 1949

beside miners and men from very different walks of life had fought side by side. Women too from different social groups had worked together in the forces or as volunteers in organisations such as the WVS and the ARP. In the late 1940s the first generation of working class children went to university and to accommodate them an extra 50,000 university places were created by 1950. Among them were men and women whose education had been interrupted

49   *Edmonton Green in 1949*

50   *The Triangle, Palmers Green*

by conscription at the age of eighteen into the armed forces. Fees were paid and each undergraduate, whose parents' income was below a certain level, received from Middlesex County Council a living allowance to cover accommodation, books and other necessities.

The monarchy too had made some changes. The King and Queen had remained in London throughout the war despite Buckingham Palace being bombed and they had visited areas such as the East End devastated by the Blitz. The King and Princess Elizabeth had make radio broadcasts and the latter had joined the ATS (the women's branch of the army) and trained as a driver/mechanic. The two Princesses had also been allowed to mingle with the crowds outside Buckingham Palace on VE night. Changes were gradually taking place which would lead to the cultural revolution ahead. The top rate of income tax was 99 per cent and this was a final blow to many landowners who could no longer afford to run their stately homes and estates. Several mansions were transferred to the National Trust and Forty Hall would soon be up for sale.

Christmas 1949 was forecast to be the best for many years with a plentiful supply of poultry (which was not rationed), beer and wine and a wide selection of toys for the children. People in each of the three boroughs looked forward optimistically to a new decade without austerity.

CHAPTER 3

The 1950s

A ndrew Marr wrote in his *History of Modern Britain* 'The Second World War had changed Britain physically and industrially, destroying city centres and encouraging immigration and emigration'. The scars of war were still apparent in 1950 in many towns of Britain, including Enfield, Edmonton and Southgate although there was some new housing on bomb sites. The 1951 census shows the population of this area at its highest ever. No census had been possible during the war so we can only compare the 1931 and 1951 figures which were:

Borough	1931	1951	% increase
Edmonton	77,658	104,224	34
Enfield	67,759	110,438	63
Southgate	56,063	73,376	31

The census also showed that there was a majority of women in this area,

51   *The Town, Enfield, in the 1950s*

1.123 for every 1,000 males. So although thousands of new houses had been built, Enfield alone had built 2,000 by 1953, there was still an acute shortage of homes. Restrictions on private building were lifted and the first priority for construction companies was to complete those developments in Nightingale Road, Edmonton, Oakwood, Winchmore Hill and other areas where dwellings had been left unfinished at the outbreak of the war. The demand for manufactured goods ensured there was almost full employment throughout the decade. Food was plentiful with only a few items still rationed and more imported items available. A report in the *Gazette* about a local woman who spent her holidays working in a camp for stateless people in Europe and the arrival of refugees, especially from Poland and Hungary escaping communist oppression, were reminders that not all were as fortunate. Indians and Cypriots arrived in significant numbers as a result of the conflicts caused by the division of their countries. Many Cypriots, both Greek and Turkish, settled in the Palmers Green area and several opened hairdressers, dry cleaners and restaurants. The Act of Parliament which had granted all Commonwealth citizens right of entry to Britain encouraged transport services, hospitals, and factories and firms short of staff to advertise overseas to fill vacancies. Rail and bus companies advertised in the West Indies for unskilled workers: many of those who responded had served with British forces during the war. The Mayor of Edmonton claimed there was no colour discrimination in Edmonton but 'No Irish, no coloureds, no dogs' notices were seen on some lodging houses until banned by the Race Discrimination Act. Emigration continued to the Commonwealth with Canada seemingly the most popular destination in the 1950s for families from this area and the newspapers contained reports back from some who had met with varying fortunes.

Although the 1950s were regarded as a welcome peaceful period after the war years, the threat of nuclear conflict cast a shadow. British troops were fighting somewhere in the world throughout the decade. In 1950 both national service conscripts and regular soldiers were involved, under the United Nations flag and alongside a wide alliance of countries, in the conflict with communist forces in Korea, the first battle of the Cold War. News of several local men was printed in the papers. Lance Corporal Richardson of Albany Park Avenue and Private William Felsted of Central Avenue wrote about the bitterly cold winter with temperatures of minus 33°F. Sergeant Heath was also in Korea, an Armourer repairing the guns of the Royal Artillery. There are reports about some who had been badly wounded and, sadly, also obituaries of local men who lost their lives in this conflict. One report in 1951 is headed 'Korean hero spends his Christmas at St Joseph's Home, Holtwhites Hill' — it seems he had lived for much of his childhood in that orphanage. The Armistice of 1953 ended this war and prisoners who were released and returned home included at least two from Enfield.

The Cold War was at its height and blighted the optimism which had been felt in the years since the war ended. 55,000 British troops were deployed along the border with communist Eastern Germany in case of a surprise attack by Soviet forces. A former pupil of Alma Road School, who was serving in the British Army of the Rhine, was awarded the BEM (British Empire Medal) in 1952. A local airman lost his life ferrying goods to Berlin during the airlift – he was on one of the 270,000 flights which carried fuel, food and other necessities to the besieged people of West Berlin. Local national service personnel

52   *Iain Macleod, MP for Enfield West*

ENFIELD WEST PARLIAMENTARY CONSTITUENCY
GENERAL ELECTION 1970

IAIN MACLEOD

YOUR CONSERVATIVE CANDIDATE

INVITES YOU TO MEET HIM AT ONE OF
HIS ELECTION MEETINGS (listed overleaf)

COME AND PUT YOUR QUESTIONS

THEN

VOTE *MACLEOD* AGAiN

on
THURSDAY, 18th JUNE

Published by J. J. M. Speed (Election Agent) 276 Baker Street Enfield and
Printed by The Galleon Press (Enfield) Ltd 4 Palace Mews, Enfield.

also served in Egypt, Libya, Kenya and Malaya. In the campaign against the communists in Malaya, Private Eric Smith of Enfield Wash saved a comrade's life and a local RAF sergeant died in battle. There was a partial rearmament at this time which benefited the arms factories of the Lea Valley and contributed to the maintenance of high employment figures but increased the national debt. The fears of many were voiced by Iain Macleod, Enfield West's MP, in 1950 when he said 'There is a real chance of a third world war at the moment'. In every locality, plans were made for civil defence and part time instructors were trained and supplied with equipment by the Home Office. In 1954 this included instructions on how to deal with an atomic explosion. St Johns Ambulance Brigade and the Red Cross provided an increased number of first aid courses and the Enfield WVS volunteers learned how to cook emergency meals in old oil drums. During the Cold War Britain needed nuclear as well as conventional weapons for defence. In January 1958 the Campaign for Nuclear Disarmament (CND) organised the first march to Aldermaston with the objective of getting Britain to ban nuclear weapons. Protest meetings and marches were also held locally but failed to stop the build-up of nuclear weapons from the USA on British soil.

National politics inevitably affected local life .The General Election of 1950 saw the Labour Party retain power but with a slender majority of five. There had been boundary changes since the 1945 election and Enfield was now divided into two constituencies, East and West. Iain Macleod, Conservative,

53   *Sir Beverley Baxter, MP with the Mayor of Southgate*

a fine orator and able politician who was to hold ministerial posts in the Conservative governments of the 1950s, was elected for the West: Graham Dalling considered him the finest MP to represent a local constituency. One of his posts was that of Colonial Secretary and he oversaw the granting of independence to several British colonies, including the first state in black Africa, Ghana. As decolonisation accelerated the local annual Empire Day celebrations were held for the last time in 1958. Ernest Davies, the former MP for the Enfield constituency was returned for Labour in Enfield East which he continued to represent until 1959. Austen Albu was again returned as Edmonton's MP. Until 1950 Southgate was part of the Wood Green constituency but this was now split and Sir Beverley Baxter, a Canadian journalist who had represented Wood Green, was elected as Southgate's first MP. All four MPs were re-elected in 1951 when the Conservatives won the general election: they confirmed their commitment to the welfare state and Winston Churchill became Prime Minister again.

Some of the problems experienced during the war continued in peacetime and one was the shortage of coal. In Enfield deliveries were five weeks behind schedule and the local papers repeated the requests of the 1940s, such as 'Please be extra careful with coal, gas and electricity to keep the factories working' while the Eastern Gas Board reported that 'Until further notice it is unable to accept orders for coke from new customers'. Twenty per cent of British industry had been nationalised by 1950 including the steel industries, coal mines, railways, British Overseas Airways Corporation and electric and

54   Shops in Church Street, Enfield, in the 1950s

gas services. The Conservative governments of the 1950s denationalised only road transport. Generous wage settlements to the 1.7 million state employees fuelled a rise in inflation to 9 per cent in 1950/1: it had been 3 per cent the previous year. The average wage in the decade was double that of 1939.

As people began to have more cash to spend shops began to fill with goods. Increasingly, however, these were imported as prices were much cheaper than home manufactured products. The introduction of hire purchase agreements on a wide scale made a big difference as people no longer had to wait to purchase furniture, household equipment and other items until they had saved the cost but could pay a deposit and then the balance by regular instalments. One shop advertised a new cooker for sale for £40 cash or £5 deposit and fifteen quarterly payment of £2 12s (£2.60) while Sylvia Roberts of Edmonton tempted ladies with offers of 'an attractive coat for winter. Pay as you wear for 8s 9d [45p] a week'. It was the beginning of the life on credit and consumerism. Purchasers were enticed by advertisements on television when the first commercial channel opened in 1955 and by the arrival of supermarkets. Sainsbury's first self-service stores opened in 1950 and encouraged shoppers to buy more than they needed. The closure of the small local shop inevitably began.

To celebrate Britain's achievements and 'for the enjoyment of all' a Festival of Britain was planned for 1951 as 'an expression of the very way of life in which we believe'. The main attractions included the Dome of Discovery, an immense display of the best of British design and manufacture, historical and scientific tableaux and modern art: this was on the South Bank of the Thames and the celebrations included a fun fair at Battersea. Over eight million people, including many from the Enfield area, visited the Festival. There were supposed to be local celebrations too but FERRA (Federation

55   *Forty Hall was purchased by Enfield Council in 1951*

56   *The Proclamation of Queen Elizabeth II was displayed outside the Public Offices,
Gentleman's Row*

57   *The Lord Mayor of London arrives to present the Charter to the Borough of Enfield*

of Enfield Ratepayers and Residents Associations) publicly criticised Enfield Council for its complete lack of any festivities. The council's response was that the acquisition of Forty Hall was intended to be a permanent memorial of the festival and that there would also be sports, entertainments and 'the tidying up of odd sites throughout the district'. Residents felt the sports and entertainments were no different from previous years and asked which sites had been improved. There was no response from the council in the papers to this question.

In February 1952 King George VI died. He had been a popular king and the local papers all led with tributes to him. Memorial services were held locally and some local shops dressed their windows in mourning colours. *The Enfield Herald* reported that 'Among the patient crowds waiting to file past the coffin in Westminster Hall have been many Enfield people, both young and old'. Police from Enfield, Southgate and Edmonton were on duty outside the hall controlling the crowds. Many also lined the route of the funeral procession and a local guardsman was one of the soldiers accompanying the gun carriage bearing the King's body. Television coverage of the funeral procession with an audience of 4.5 million is credited with alerting the public to the miracle of this medium and the consequent increase in the sale of sets. Copies of the proclamation of the new monarch, Queen Elizabeth II, were displayed by all the Councils; Enfield's was placed outside the Public Offices at 1 Gentleman's Row. People looked forward hopefully to a new Elizabethan Age as did the Prime Minister who said in the House of Commons 'Let us hope and pray the accession of Queen Elizabeth will be a signal of a brightening salvation of the human race'.

Events in 1952 which were reported include that in the Olympic Games a member of Southgate Harriers, Peter Higgins, won a bronze medal in the 440 yards and that Enfield Urban District Council, at last, petitioned the Queen for borough status. Southgate had been a borough since 1933 and Edmonton since 1937 but Enfield had remained an Urban District Council. Since the 1930s there had been discussions about a change of status but arguments over boundaries and then the war had delayed action. In November 1954 the Privy Council invited Enfield UDC to prepare a draft charter and the Queen approved this in March 1955. Charter day was 27 September 1955 when the Lord Mayor of London handed over the Charter of Incorporation to the Mayor of Enfield to the accompaniment of a trumpet fanfare. A civic lunch was held at the Grammar School followed by a service at St Andrew's Church. It was a day of pageantry and civic pride and crowds thronged the streets to see the procession of horse drawn carriages on their way to Forty Hall but all were unaware that Enfield's status as a separate borough was destined to last for only ten years. A new town hall was considered a top priority as the UDC's principal offices were still housed at 1 Gentleman's Row which had long been inadequate and the overflow of officers was found in temporary accommodation around the town. A site in Silver Street had been earmarked and an architectural competition in 1957 resulted in the selection of a young architect, Eric Broughton. Building began on the first stage which included the council chamber, committee rooms and some offices. The estimated cost was £759,000. The Labour Party was successful in the first election for the new borough and remained in power throughout the 1950s in both Enfield and Edmonton. In Southgate the main party in power was in reality Conservative but had always been called Independent, sponsored by the ratepayers and similar organisations. In 1951 the Independent candidates were challenged by those from the official Conservative Party, only one of whom was successful at this election. However, Conservative candidates gradually won more seats in local elections and this resulted later in the end of non-party candidates.

In November 1952 the London area was covered by a dense smog, caused by weather conditions and pollution. The local hospitals were busy with patients suffering breathing problems and there were some deaths. Extra ambulances were deployed but they took three to four hours to do journeys which would normally have taken thirty minutes. The fog was so thick it was impossible to see more than two or three yards ahead and traffic ground to a standstill. The last scheduled bus arrived at the Ponders End Garage at 4am and seventeen stranded people spent the night at Enfield Police Station. As a result of the high level of pollution the Government introduced the Clean Air Act by which houses and factories in the London area were forbidden to burn coal or other polluting fuels. Local councils had to enforce this law and ensure all homes and industrial premises used smokeless fuel, gas or electricity. Southgate began its campaign in the Cockfosters area but Enfield's plans were delayed when it was discovered that no smokeless fuel was on sale in that borough. At this time central heating was very rare in private houses.

The coronation of Queen Elizabeth II in 1953 was seen by many people as a boundary between a grey past and a colourful future. The local shopping centres and some streets and factories were decorated and buildings, including Ponders End Flour Mills and St Andrew's church, were floodlit. The decorations on Southgate Green included three brass balls which provoked questions in the *Palmers Green & Southgate Gazette* about their significance but the councillor responsible admitted he had no idea. A major change from the past was the first televising of the ceremony so that viewers could see it live. There was an unprecedented sale of television sets with an audience estimated to have been 27 million. Edmonton Council set up screens in the Town Hall for those who did not have access to sets. All enjoyed the pomp and ceremony as did the two million lining the streets of Central London, despite the rain. Among them was a group of Albany School boys who had tickets for seats on the route. Other local people were there among the military lining the route, staffing the St John's Ambulance and Red Cross First Aid stations and

58   *The Coronation decorations on The Green, Southgate provoked criticism*

59 & 60   Coronation celebrations

61 & 62   *Coronation Gates and plaque,*
Broomfield Park

an 11-year-old from Palmers Green who was a chorister at Westminster Abbey.
There were local celebrations which continued for a week. Many streets had
parties and there was dancing in the parks, fireworks, a gymkhana, sports
competitions, performances of 'Merrie England' and many other activities.
Coronation gates were planned by Southgate Council for Broomfield Park as
it was also its golden jubilee. Southgate schoolchildren received replicas of
the anointing spoon used in the coronation ceremony, except for the infants

63   *Shakespeare Cottages were among the old buildings demolished*

who were given propelling pencils. People's spirits were raised not only by
the coronation but because 1953 finally saw the end of rationing and utility
furniture and clothing. There was pride in British recent achievements which
included the first conquest of Mount Everest, the discovery of the structure
of DNA by scientists who were subsequently awarded the Nobel Prize, the
launch of the world's first passenger jet liner, the Comet, and in 1954 Roger
Bannister's world record of running a mile in under four minutes.

     For many living on the East Coast, however, 1953 was a grim year as floods
destroyed homes and livelihoods. Seventy people from Canvey Island sought
refuge with friends and families in Enfield, while others stayed in Edmonton
and other areas. Distress funds were set up by all the Councils to raise money
for them. The three branches of the WVS organised collections of clothes,
bedding, toys and other goods for people who had lost everything and five
lorry loads were sent from Enfield. Local fire engines went to assist the hard
pressed Essex Fire Brigade,

     During the 1950s many historic buildings, such as the Village Hall and
Shakespeare Cottages, Southgate, and the Victorian Enfield Collegiate School
in London Road were razed to make way for new offices or housing. Because
of high taxation owners of stately homes were finding it increasingly difficult
to maintain their mansions and so Enfield UDC purchased Forty Hall for
£41,000. A Conservative councillor called it 'A complete white elephant' and
it was initially turned into flats with limited access to the gardens and park
for the general public. Myddelton House in Bulls Cross was bought by the
University of London School of Pharmacy. Stately homes in other regions,
such as Woburn Abbey, opened their doors to paying visitors and outings by
coach to historic houses began to appear in the lists of day trips arranged by
local coach companies.

64   Myddelton House

The founding of the Enfield Archaeological Society in 1955 resulted in increased knowledge of the past becoming available. The first excavations were of Roman settlements in the area but the Society's most notable work was the discovery of part of Elsyng Palace, a former royal residence, in the grounds of Forty Hall.

Many people were dismayed by the destruction of our heritage and by

65   The Rose & Crown public house

66   St Andrew's Church

67 (above)   Gentleman's Row

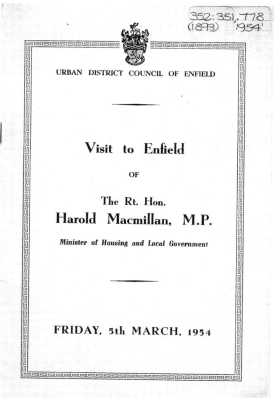

352:351,778
(1893) 1954

URBAN DISTRICT COUNCIL OF ENFIELD

Visit to Enfield

OF

The Rt. Hon.

Harold Macmillan, M.P.

Minister of Housing and Local Government

FRIDAY, 5th MARCH, 1954

*68 (left)   Programme for
Harold Macmillan's visit to the
Angel Road development*

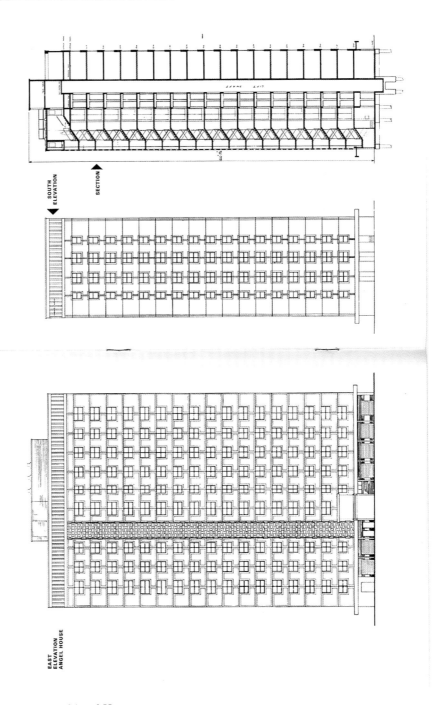

69   *Drawings of Angel House*

70 Angel House tower block

1959 buildings of historical or architectural interest were listed and their future protection assured. The Minister of Planning issued a list of 'gems of architecture preserved for posterity' which included Myddelton House, Capel Manor, the Rose & Crown, Forty Hall, St Andrew's Church and houses in Forty Hill and Gentleman's Row and on Southgate and Winchmore Hill Greens. Tree preservation orders were similarly introduced, one of the first being to prevent the cutting down of five trees at Oakwood Station.

Life in 1954 was made difficult at times by a series of wild-cat strikes by dockers, railway workers, bus employees and others. Trade union power rose considerably with most workers belonging to the appropriate union and wage settlements were in double figures. The housing shortage, however, eased as the Conservative Government had made housing a priority and 340,000 new homes had been built nationwide by that year. One development at Angel Road, Edmonton, was visited by the then Minister of Housing, Harold Macmillan who became Prime Minister three years later. Enfield was virtually fully developed and so attempted to build 2,500 homes at Little Amwell in Hertfordshire but the application was opposed by Ware Council. Southgate's proposal to build houses on playing fields was also withdrawn because of local opposition. Many large Edwardian houses in areas such as The Ridgeway, Bycullah Road Enfield, Bush Hill Park and Chase Road Southgate were either demolished and replaced by blocks of apartments or converted into flats. The major area being re-developed at this time was New Southgate with the district's first tower blocks.

Overseas travel restrictions were lifted and many people went abroad for the first time in their lives. Holidays in Switzerland, France and other countries were prominent among the adverts in the press. In the early 1950s travel to Europe was usually by ferry and train but as air travel gradually became cheaper and more frequent some people ventured further afield to America, Australia and South Africa. There were also more visitors from overseas including business men visiting local factories, sports teams, civic dignitaries, schoolchildren and others both to and from this area as part of Town Twinning.

The age of the car began in 1950. Car ownership had quadrupled by 1959 and adverts for Hillman, Morris, Riley, Austin and other British manufacturers appeared weekly in the local newspapers. As a consequence of the increase in traffic there were more reports of road accidents and local casualties, especially cyclists. During the 1950s the first motorways were built and the first parking meters and yellow lines appeared on the streets.

There was, inevitably, a downside to the prosperity. Increased vandalism is reported in every edition of all the local papers, such as damage to 710 street lamps in Enfield, to play equipment in parks, churches and trees throughout the decade. Residents Associations highlighted problems in their areas such as the 'disgraceful behaviour' in Fore Street, Edmonton 'where shopkeepers were having to put up with every kind of annoyance by groups of young louts and girls'. Edmonton Petty Sessions reported an increasing amount of juvenile delinquency

In the mid-1950s Britain was still a world player, the second richest country in the world and a global leader in shipping and finance. In a biography of Hugh Gaitskell, the Leader of the Labour Party from 1955, it was stated that 'Britain was changing, growing more affluent and beginning to enjoy the peace'. The peace was, however, to be shattered briefly by the Suez fiasco of 1956. President Nasser had nationalised the Anglo-French Suez Canal and British and French troops were sent to Egypt. A local RAF flight-lieutenant lost his life, one of the twenty-one servicemen killed in the action. Britain and France were forced to withdraw ignominiously by a United Nations ultimatum which was backed by the United States. One of the results of the conflict was a severe shortage of petrol which was rationed as it has been during the war. Half of Europe's oil supplies from the Middle East had been transported through the Suez Canal as had a quarter of Britain's exports and imports. The Suez campaign had the support of less than half the British public and a protest against the Anglo-French action was organised by Enfield Labour Party.

In 1941 George Orwell had written 'The war, unless we are defeated, will wipe out most of the existing class privileges'. During the war not only had thousands of small houses been destroyed but also several mansions, part of Buckingham Palace and the London Guildhall. J. B. Priestley said in one of his popular radio talks 'This country had been bombed into democracy'. Men from all walks of life had fought side by side and those who followed them would continue to do so as teenage national service troops. Mary Churchill (later Lady Soames), who was in the ATS, said 'Uniform is a tremendous leveller. We all looked the same, lovely girls from Liverpool and country bumpkins like me'. While there was none of the hollow rhetoric, which in 1918 had promised 'a land fit for heroes', after the war people expected a decent home, good free education and proper medical care. In the 1950s some of these aspirations became a reality for many. 30,000 more students were going to university, more good housing was available and the National Health Service was free for everyone.

Several changes in the law reflected a change in moral attitudes. Society in the early 1950s Britain was still a conformist society with a climate of suspicion that all homosexuals were traitors, spies or security risks, a view that was encouraged by the defection of the soviet spies Burgess, Maclean and Philby in 1951. However a change resulted from the report of the Wolfenden Committee in 1954. Until 1957 homosexuals were prosecuted and there are several reports in the local papers of charges in the courts of 'gross indecency' resulting in imprisonment. The 1957 Act legalised private homosexual acts between consenting adults over twenty-one years of age. Capital punishment was also abolished and the law on abortion amended to allow termination in certain conditions.

Iain Macleod, Enfield West's MP, said at the end of the 1950s 'People are enjoying a prosperity beyond our dreams'. However, it had not been a decade without problems which would recur during the coming years. Britain was not producing enough and too much had been spent on defence and not enough on modernisation and this would severely affect production in the factories of the Lea Valley.

London had grown enormously since the last local government reorganisation of 1889 when the London County Council had been set up to administer what was then the London conurbation. It now spilled over into parts of Kent, Surrey and Essex and virtually the whole of Middlesex. A Royal Commission recommended the establishment of a Greater London Authority which would become a reality in the 1960s.

CHAPTER 4

The 1960s

This decade was a noisy one of protest, free speech, civil rights and lively music. It has become known as The Swinging Sixties on account of the reduction of social taboos and the arrival of a new age of 'pop' music such as rock 'n' roll. Britain led the world in popular culture with groups such as the Beatles. London became the international fashion capital and although the latter was centred on the Kings Road, Chelsea and Carnaby Street, its influence was felt in Outer London. The 1960s have come to be regarded as the era of a generation which had not experienced the poverty of the 1930s or the strain of the war years and these young people set the trend for the rest of the twentieth century. They no longer dressed like their parents and local shops such as the Shindy Boutique in Enfield had 'all the latest gear',

71   Teddy boys

72 The author with her scooter and godson

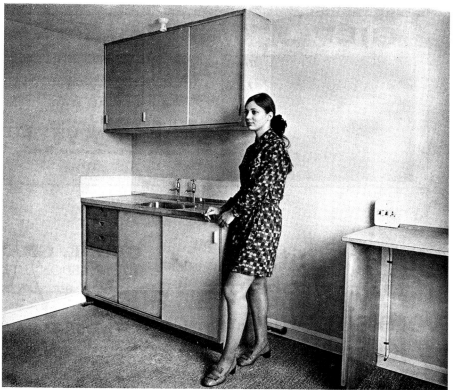

73 A mini-skirted girl in a modern kitchen

while another, 'Carnaby Street comes to Enfield', stocked the newest fashions. The Young Fashionables in Fore Street, Edmonton, advertised 'young guy clothes' which doubtless included the drainpipe trousers and long jackets favoured by some young men. Those who dressed in this fashion came to be called Teddy Boys. The Hippies wore kaftans and beads while the division between the Mods and the Rockers was apparent from their style of dress. Scooters, especially Vespas and Lambrettas, were popular and scooter clubs were set up in both Enfield and Edmonton. The Rockers preferred motor bikes. Advertisements for both types of vehicle were advertised regularly in the local papers. Girls wore copies of the mini-skirts created by Mary Quant for her Kings Road boutique. The majority of teenagers left school at 15 with no qualifications but in this period of full employment they had money and enjoyed themselves in very different ways from their parents' generation. Not everyone approved: the novelist, Barbara Cartland, in a talk at Winchmore Hill, attacked 'the immorality of Swinging London'. Pop groups attracted hundreds of screaming fans, mostly teenage mini-skirted girls, to venues such as the Regal Cinema, Edmonton when the Rolling Stones performed there, and many travelled to neighbouring Tottenham when in July 1964 the Beatles sang in a night club.

It was the decade of liberalisation. The caning of children and flogging of prisoners was made illegal, the death penalty was abolished, divorce became simpler — the rate almost doubled between 1965 and 1970 — and there were changing attitudes to abortion and homosexuality. Sexual liberalisation resulted from the availability from 1962 of the contraceptive pill. This especially affected women who, after the immediate post-war years when they had concentrated on running the home and raising children, now returned to earn a living by working in offices and factories and they enjoyed spending their own money and being less dependent on their husbands. There was also a 'cultural revolution in the arts'. Theatre censorship was abolished and publishing was liberated when in 1960 Penguin Books, at the Old Bailey, defeated the charge of obscenity and published the novel *Lady Chatterley's Lover*. Pop art dominated the fine arts scene and artists such as Bridget Riley came to be taken seriously. Programmes of political satire began to be broadcast on radio and television: 'That Was The Week That Was' and 'Mrs Wilson's Diary' parodied previous sacrosanct subjects such as parliament, the church, the monarchy and the law. At its peak TWTW, as it came to be called, had 12 million viewers. No subject was taboo so the class system, illegitimacy and race relations were for the first time discussed on air and contributed to a challenging attitude towards authority and a declining lack of respect for age. Pop music dominated the music scene and local dance halls, public houses and bars resounded to the sounds of rock 'n' roll which provoked frequent complaints about the noise in the letters section of the local newspapers. Bowes Park Methodist Church was one of the places advertising an evening of 'pop music with space for jiving'. Coffee bars with juke boxes, the haunt of the young, were opened in many places such as a former air raid shelter at Lacey Hall, Palmers Green, but there were protests from local residents about proposals to open more. The demand for regulation of opening hours because of the noise and late closing of a coffee bar in Oakwood led the Southgate MP, Anthony Berry, to ask a question in the House of Commons about licensing such premises but it was not until March 1968 that local

74   *Georgian cottages, Southgate Green*

councils were given new powers to control the opening hours of cafes and coffee bars.

Both 1962 and 1963 began with blizzards, snow and freezing temperatures. However the councils were better prepared to cope with the snow than in 1952 and main roads were cleared quickly. Football matches and other sporting fixtures were cancelled for two months and there were power failures. At least one pensioners' Christmas party was held by candlelight. Also in 1963 traffic chaos was caused by the worst fog blackout for ten years.

1962 was the year of the birth of Southgate Civic Society, largely as a response to the threat to demolish the Georgian cottages on Southgate Green. Its aims were : 'to promote the study of civic change: to stimulate public consciousness and appreciation of the beauty, history and character of the neighbourhood: to encourage the preservation, development and improvement of the features which go to make a pleasing and convenient condition in which to work and live: to call attention when desirable to any activities or proposals affecting the interest of residents and to create opportunities for the expression of public opinion: to pursue these actions by meetings, exhibitions, publications and the formation of study groups.' The subscription was fixed at 7s 6d (37.5p). Early activities included bulb and tree planting in parts of the Borough.

In 1964 the restrictive practice of resale price maintenance was abolished and this allowed retailers to set their own prices on goods for sale. Jack Cohen, the founder of Tesco, had lobbied for this change and, as a result,

75 & 76   *Southgate Civic Society planting bulbs and trees*

77 (right)   The former
vicarage of St Mary Magdalene

78 (below)   Sir Anthony Berry
MP in New Southgate

79   Crowds
gathered round the
world's first ATM
on Barclays Bank,
Enfield

supermarkets began to discount items for sale. More supermarkets appeared in all areas and small shops started to close.

Christopher Bray, in his recently published (2014) book, *1965 — The Year Modern Britain Was Born*, suggests that 'this was the year everything changed, the year that blew away the hidebound Britain that preceded it and gave us the country we have today' — it was the start of the so called Permissive Society. Drugs became more easily available and reports of court cases for possession of illegal substances were more frequent as was, sadly, the occasional death of a young victim. The Enfield Education Committee discussed the problem of drugs in schools. The Vicar of Christ Church, Southgate, in a sermon referred to 'teenage drug-takers'. The former vicarage of St Mary Magdalene was taken over by the Moral Welfare Association as a home for unmarried mothers and their babies.

Outside decisions and events which affected life in the Enfield area included the 1962 Commonwealth Immigration Act which restricted entry to Britain, except for the Irish, and so in 1961 to beat the ban there was an influx of Commonwealth citizens. Later the main immigration was from East Africa, especially Asians from Kenya where they had been deprived of jobs in the civil service and the right to trade. Many bought shops, especially newsagents. The first Race Relations Act became law in 1965. The coming of the breathalyser and the introduction of the 70mph speed limit reduced the number of road accidents. National Service for young men ceased. One major scandal, the Profumo Affair, which almost caused the collapse of the Conservative Government in 1963, was brushed aside by Southgate MP Anthony Berry, who said 'the sooner they put the whole matter into perspective and start to think again about the events that really matter, the better'.

Britain was not involved in the war in Vietnam. However, there were anti-war protests from many organisations such as the Enfield Co-operative Women's Guild and students unions at Enfield College. Demonstrations against nuclear weapons continued throughout the next decade. Flags on buildings were flown at half mast in 1965 to mark the death of Sir Winston Churchill and the papers printed tributes to him. Local residents were among the 300,000 who filed past his coffin in Westminster Hall where it lay in state for three days.

The devaluation of the pound in November 1967 by 14 per cent increased the cost of imported goods and overseas holidays, although it was hoped it would lead to improved export figures for local factories. Austen Albu, Edmonton's MP, said publicly that in his opinion the devaluation should have been much earlier.

Sir Beverley Baxter announced early in 1964 that he would not be standing again at the next General Election and he died shortly before it took place. Sir Anthony Berry was elected to replace him: (he remained Southgate's MP until 1984 when he was killed in the IRA attack on the Conservative Party conference hotel in Brighton). The other MPs were re-elected to parliament: Iain Macleod for Enfield West, Austen Albu for Edmonton and John Mackie for Enfield East. The following year the Conservative Party for the first time elected its leader by a ballot of MPs. Edward Heath was chosen, the first grammar school educated politician to hold this office and the first to have no aristocratic connections.

Real public concern at the state of the green belt in Enfield was expressed in the late 1960s. The number of derelict sites led to suggestions that they had been 'neglected in order to get planning permission'. FERRA (Federation of Enfield Ratepayers and Residents Associations) organised a 'Hands off the Green Belt' campaign and was pleased when plans for a development of shops and housing at Crews Hill were rejected by the Minister of Housing and Local Government.

The 1960s were a decade of technological advances: in 1966 computers began to be advertised for sale locally and some local firms recruited clerical officers to operate them. The council also started to use computers in areas such as planning. The manual telephone exchanges were replaced by automatic ones. Surprisingly, the world's first ever ATM (automated teller machine) was installed in the front wall of Barclays Bank, Enfield Town. The Russians had initiated the space age with the launch of the first man-made satellite, Sputnik, in 1959 and the flight in space of the first man, Yuri Gagarin, in 1961. At the end of this decade American astronauts walked on the moon. Edmonton could claim some of the glory as Dr J. Hodge, Chief of the Advanced Mission Programme at the Manned Spacecraft Centre in Houston, Texas, grew up in Forest Road, Edmonton and was educated at Houndsfield, Enfield Grammar and Minchenden Schools. Other local men made a contribution to space exploration, one was an electrical mechanic in the crew testing ballistic missiles and another was appointed Deputy Head of Mullard Space Science Laboratory.

Three issues dominated the local papers in the 1960s. First, there was the council's proposal to build a ring road round the centre of Enfield, through the ancient churchyard, the Grammar School playing fields, Holly Walk and

80   The new coat-of-arms
for the London Borough of
Enfield

81   Miss K. Harvey, first mayor of the new borough

82   Fir Tree House was demolished and replaced by Civic Centre offices

over the New River. The Enfield Preservation Society took a leading role in
opposing the scheme, which was finally rejected. This campaign is described
in Chapter 10, 'Enfield Preservation Society'. The second major controversy
centred on the coming of comprehensive education. Again there were lengthy
campaigns and protests, especially from some parents of boys at Enfield
Grammar School and this is covered in Chapter 8, 'Education'.

The third issue was the result of the reorganisation of local government
on the lines recommended in 1960 by the Royal Commission. The proposal
was for the enlargement of the London area to include parts of Kent, Essex
and Surrey and almost the whole of Middlesex. Middlesex County Council

83 Portcullis House stood on the site of the tower block of the Civic Centre

was to be abolished and a new authority, the Greater London Council set up. The newspapers contained many letters, both for and against the change. Sir Beverley Baxter, MP for Southgate, said the new structure left him 'shocked and horrified' while others predicted 'years of disruption'. Existing district councils were to be amalgamated into larger units called London Boroughs. The first suggested combinations were Edmonton and Tottenham, Southgate and Hornsey, Enfield and Cheshunt. However in 1963, after much discussion, it was agreed that Edmonton, Enfield and Southgate should form Borough 32 with a population of 275,000 residents. Cheshunt remained in Hertfordshire and Potters Bar was transferred to that county. There were to be thirty electoral wards in the new borough and each would elect two councillors. Ideas for a name were invited and among the suggestions were Southeden and Edengate but when it was decided in early 1964 that the new borough offices should be in Enfield, the decision was taken to retain that name. Local historians commented that the union of the three boroughs revived an historic link dating back to the days of the Edmonton Hundred. A new coat-of-arms was agreed, after some argument, to include the Edmonton lion, the Southgate stag and the mythical Enfield beast. The first election to the new council was held in 1964

84 *Opening of the first section of the new Civic Centre*

85   *The first new section of the Civic Centre*

86   Edmonton Councillors and residents at the Farewell Dinner in April 1965

87   WVS Meals on Wheels

and resulted in a narrow win for the Labour Party with thirty-one councillors to the Conservatives twenty-nine. The first Mayor of the London Borough of Enfield was Miss K. Harvey. Staff from the three previous administrations were appointed to senior posts: the new Borough Treasurer, Education Officer, Housing Manager and Borough Engineer were transferred from Edmonton Council while the Town Clerk, Medical Officer, Librarian and Park Superintendent were from Enfield. One of the first priorities was the building of offices for the new authority and it was decided to use the site in Silver Street. An architectural competition resulted in the acceptance of a design by Eric Broughton. The first stage of a new Civic Centre was planned to incorporate a council chamber, committee rooms and some offices. Despite many misgivings the feeling in 1966 was that the new borough was working better than many had anticipated and the public was pleased that GLC rates were lower than many had expected. However, the closed shop policy of the former Enfield and Edmonton Councils, whereby all employees had to be members of an appropriate union, was continued and this led to a protest in 1966 by local builders who joined together to fight the ruling that they could only employ workers belonging to a trade union on council projects and contracts. Only Edmonton is reported as having organised a celebration to bid farewell to the former Borough Council when in April 1965 a dinner dance was attended by councillors and local residents.

Housing was a priority for the new council. At the time of the amalgamation, Southgate had thirteen housing schemes planned from New Southgate to Winchmore Hill and in 1968 the first high rise flats in New Southgate were occupied. The Minister of Housing gave permission for residential development on nursery land in Chase Road, Southgate. The building of four blocks of twelve-storey flats and seven blocks of maisonettes on land between Ordnance Road and Turkey Brook was agreed but ninety houses had to be demolished. John Mackie, MP for Enfield East, complained in the House of Commons about the poor housing in which so many people lived in his constituency. Tower blocks were proposed for Ponders End to improve this situation but the ones built on Lavender Hill, Enfield, met with local opposition. Ross McWhirter, Conservative parliamentary candidate for Edmonton, also called for a housing crusade to speed up the building of new homes to replace the slums in that part of the new Borough. The abolished Edmonton Council, meanwhile, had won two Civic Trust Awards for the design of its Potters Bar estate and of the shops and housing development at Alpha Road. In July 1965 a 'revolutionary technique in council flat building' was employed in Angel House, a seventeen-storey block of flats in Edmonton, using an on-site vertical casting technique. Confirmation that many new homes were being built came in January 1967 from the Minister of Housing, Anthony Greenwood, who congratulated the LBE on the completion of its ten-thousandth new home.

Another problem for the new councillors was the ageing population with an increasing number of people over 65 and the consequent strain on resources. Services 'for the old' at Ruth Winston House, Palmers Green were increased and special housing units were built, some of them in the grounds of local churches, such as St Johns, Green Lanes, Palmers Green, All Saints, Edmonton and Christ Church, Enfield. New clubs for the retired were set up and were so popular that there were waiting lists to join many of them. In

88 & 89   Winchmore Hill Green before and after the demolition of shops

90   Houses in Powys Lane, Southgate, prior to demolition

91   Enfield Town was the first conservation area

92   *Forty Hall in the Forty Hill Conservation Area*

1967 Edmonton WRVS (previously called the WVS) reported that they had delivered 30,000 meals on wheels in a year.

In July 1966 Enfield Council allocated £4 million for the building of a new shopping and leisure centre with tower block housing at Edmonton Green and this development was approved by the Minister of Housing and Local Government in December. Construction began in 1968. Funds were also earmarked for the restoration of Forty Hall.

1968 was a year of local protests. The first one recorded was in January when nearly 200 'English style Red Guards' stormed into the Angel Centre, Raynton Road, Edmonton to make an inflammatory attack on the Government and its leaders, bearing banners 'Down with Wilson' and 'Down with local MPs'. Then in March there was uproar in the gallery at a council meeting when sixty angry residents demonstrated about the fear of a health hazard from the dust coming from the cement works at the bottom of Rays Road, Edmonton, and demanded new homes or closure of the works. In May there was a further protest about the lack of action when protestors closed the street.

Vandalism and anti-social behaviour continued to increase. Racism was still evident in the first years of this decade; three youths were in court in 1960 for writing 'Death to the Jews' on a fence at Bush Hill Park Station and local firms were criticised publicly for their reluctance to employ 'coloured school leavers'. The Race Relations Act of 1965 outlawed any colour bar in public places and services and incitement to racial hatred became a crime. As a result of vandalism, twenty homes in Edmonton had no electricity for two days. *The Tottenham & Edmonton Herald* reported that in January 1964 youth

93 Southgate Green Conservation Area

94   Winchmore Hill Green Conservation Area

clubs in Edmonton had to be closed because of 'teenage gang raids' and, in that same year, Edmonton Council warned ratepayers that their bill for rates would increase because of 'vandalism by hooligans and wanton destruction' at Edmonton Green.

Demolition of historic buildings continued including the Queen Anne Hill House on Church Hill, Winchmore Hill, the eighteenth-century fire station in Little Park Gardens, Enfield, shops on Winchmore Hill Green and the Old Bakery, Forty Hill. The cottages on Southgate Green were saved by the Civic Amenities Act of 1968 but two houses in Powys Lane were demolished because they were said to be in a bad state of repair. This provoked Southgate Civic Society to write 'This Society believes that a too-enthusiastic quest for tidiness may not always be beneficial to the pattern of the neighbourhood'. Edmonton lost many buildings and in April 1968 the *Palmers Green & Southgate Gazette* reported 'Move to save Edmonton buildings. Members of the Enfield Preservation Society, Southgate Civic Society and Edmonton Hundred Historical Society met to discuss the problem of preserving Edmonton's few remaining buildings of architectural value'. It was hoped that the creation of the first conservation areas would halt such destruction. The first areas to be designated in 1968 were Enfield Town, Forty Hill, Southgate Green and Winchmore Hill Green.

'Enfield defies the national swing' was the headline when in the General Election of 1966. Iain Macleod was returned for Enfield West with an increased majority while the Labour Party under Harold Wilson won many Conservative seats elsewhere. There were many difficulties ahead — strikes by dustmen, teachers and many others caused problems for all while the omens for the future of British industry were not auspicious. Britain's industrial output grew more slowly than other comparable nations and its share of world trade was shrinking. One event in that year, however, brought joy to many when England defeated Germany at Wembley and won the Football World Cup.

The Tottenham & Edmonton Weekly Herald announced in 1966 that local historians were unhappy at a plan for a new society,' The Edmonton History Association', as they felt it would lead to overlapping membership and duplication of activity with the long established Edmonton Hundred Historical Society. After some investigation by reporters, who could not trace the named officers of the proposed new society, the Chairman of EHHS, David Avery, called it 'a fantastic hoax'.

By the end of the 1960s Britain was a post-industrial and multi-ethnic society. The majority of the people were wealthier, better housed, fed and educated than ever before. Tastes had become more cosmopolitan and Indian and Chinese restaurants replaced some fish and chip shops. Many people went abroad for their annual holiday rather than to British resorts. Education had increased the flow of working class children through grammar school into universities and on to jobs in the professions, resulting in increased social mobility. Comprehensive education became the norm and many private schools closed. Leisure activities changed with the arrival of the age of consumerism and shopping became a very popular pastime while membership of political parties and church attendance declined. Britain had altered greatly in the previous thirty years. Most of the changes were here to stay and they form the basis of today's society.

CHAPTER 5

Leisure

Chambers Dictionary defines leisure as 'time away from work, freedom from occupation' but during the war there was little free time. Most men and women who were not in the armed services volunteered, when their working day ended, to drive ambulances, fire watch for incendiary bombs on office and factory roofs or serve with the Fire Service, the Home Guard, the ARP (Air Raid Precautions), WVS (Women's Voluntary Service), Red Cross, St John's Ambulance Brigade or one of the other organisations which supported the war effort on the home front. In the so-called 'phoney war', the period

95   *Regal Cinema, Edmonton*

96 & 97   The Alcazar Cinema, Edmonton, before and after bombing in 1940

between the declaration of war and the blitz on London, some ARP members found they had some spare time so they organised entertainments, dances, children's parties and other social activities in their neighbourhoods. At the Lamb Institute in Edmonton this included a production of Noel Coward's play *Hay Fever.*

When people did have a few free hours their major leisure activity was going to the cinema. At the outbreak of World War ll all cinemas were closed briefly, but the local ones, except the Plaza Ponders End, had re-opened by the end of September 1939. The Alcazar, Edmonton was, however, destroyed in a bombing raid in 1940 and the Florida, Enfield was damaged in another raid and was used as a Ministry of Food depot until 1947, when it re-opened as a cinema. There were, however, many other cinemas which provided entertainment throughout the war years. The facilities varied from the basic so-called 'flea pits' to lavish theatres seating 2,000-3,000 such as the Regal, Edmonton, one of five mammoth cinemas built in Middlesex, and the Savoy, Enfield, which had ballrooms, cafés, lifts, car parks and sometimes staged theatrical performances, organ recitals and live concerts in addition

98   *Children's programmes were enjoyed at the Odeon, Southgate and other cinemas*

to screening films. The normal programme consisted of two feature films, trailers for the next programme and a newsreel, which provoked boos from the audience whenever Hitler appeared on the screen. Most of the films were American black-and-white imports such as *Casablanca* but a few, including *Gone with the Wind*, were in colour. In 1940 the Ministry of Information took over the GPO Film Unit and produced a major series of documentaries which were often screened between the feature films. Some of these such as *London Can Take It* were intended to boost morale, while others, *Salvage with a Smile* and *More Eggs from your Hens*, offered practical advice on helping the war effort. A few British feature films were also produced to encourage patriotism including Noel Coward's *In Which We Serve* and Laurence Olivier's *Henry V*.

Cinema goers were warned of air raids by a notice which was flashed on to the screen — 'We have to inform our patrons that an air raid alert has just sounded. Will those of you who wish to leave the cinema please do so now'. In August 1940 the film at the Edmonton Empire was interrupted by such a notice with the additional information that a German bomber had been shot down over Edmonton. The audience cheered and many left the cinema to join the sightseers in the streets. Cinemas continued to provide the main leisure activity in the post-war years of the 1950s. The British film industry was revived and Ealing comedies such as *Passport to Pimlico, Whisky Galore* and *Kind Hearts and Coronets* were popular and made people laugh at a time when life was difficult and gloomy in many ways. Sir Michael Balcon, head of Ealing Studios, said he wanted these films to show Britain as a leader in social reform and a champion of social liberty. In many the heroes were working class, the villains were 'posh' and the importance of the little man standing up to bullies was often demonstrated. So shopkeepers challenged Whitehall officials and little old ladies outwitted criminal gangs. There were also other excellent classic British films such as *Great Expectations* and *Brief Encounter* made in this period. In 1948 local churches led the opposition to the opening of cinemas on Sundays but, after a long debate, it was finally agreed. There were special programmes for children on Saturday mornings at many venues, including the Rialto in Enfield Town and the Odeon, Southgate.

In the 1950s cinema attendance began to decline as more households acquired television sets. In 1947 only two of every hundred British households had a TV set but this figure had risen to seventy by 1957. There was a surge in sales in 1953 when it was announced that the Queen's Coronation would be shown live. The cinemas which closed in this decade were the New Coronation, New Southgate, the Capitol, Winchmore Hill, the Queens and Palmadium, Palmers Green, the Hippodrome and Grenada, Edmonton and the Premier, Hertford Road, Enfield. Some were converted into bingo halls but many were demolished. A few, including the Regal, Edmonton and the Savoy, Enfield, were converted into multiplexes with several smaller studio cinemas. By 1970 there were only six left in the London Borough of Enfield: the Regal, Edmonton, Ritz, Bowes Road, New Southgate, the Odeon, Southgate, the Savoy, Florida and Rialto Enfield and most of those did not survive for much longer.

From 1959 there was a change in the type of British film produced. Working-class realism in, for example, *I'm All Right Jack* replaced escapism in films such as *Maytime in Mayfair*. They were often set in the North or Midlands: *Room at the Top* in Yorkshire and *Saturday Night and Sunday Morning* in Nottingham and the leading man was usually a manual worker. Locally in 1959 *The Inn of the Sixth Happiness* about an Edmonton girl, Gladys Aylward, proved popular as did *To Russia with Love*, the first James Bond film in 1960.

Church attendances across all denominations began to decline. The Minister of Palmers Green Baptist Church warned of 'a pagan nation in danger'. The Methodist churches reported a decrease in the number of children attending Sunday School and some church buildings which had been bombed were not replaced, However there were some exceptions, as the Roman Catholic Church on London Road was rebuilt and the new Progressive Synagogue opened in Chase Road, Southgate. The arrival of immigrants from the West Indies in the 1950s resulted in the opening of a new type of evangelical church, while groups of different faiths built mosques and Sikh and Hindu temples to serve their communities.

The second most popular leisure activity throughout the 1940s and 1950s was dancing. Every Saturday night there were long queues outside the Royalty Dance Hall in Winchmore Hill Road and other venues, including Church House, Southgate, St Paul's Institute and Firs Hall, Winchmore Hill. In the summer there were open air dances in Ponders End Recreation Ground, Hilly Fields, Pymmes and other parks. Music was provided by local bands such as Jo Hart's and the favourite dances were the waltz, quickstep and tango. American influence led to the jive, rock 'n' roll, the twist and other modern dances being preferred in the 1950s. As reported in Chapter 1, the Princes Dance Hall, Palmers Green was one of the most popular venues until it was destroyed in a bombing raid.

The BBC television service was suspended during the war but radio played a key role in keeping the population at home advised of developments in the war, providing entertainment and maintaining morale. There were special programmes such as 'Bombers over Germany' which described an RAF raid on a German oil refinery, music, sport, Children's Hour, advice on health and stirring speeches from the Prime Minister and others. The restrictions on travel and the blackout led most families to stay at home during the evenings and many played card games: Monopoly, Lexicon and whist were popular and, later, Scrabble produced by the Enfield firm, J. W. Spears & Sons.

Regular live theatre performances were enjoyed at the Intimate Theatre in St Monica's Church Hall, Green Lanes. It had a wide repertoire and a different production every week. Like the cinemas, all theatres were closed for a few weeks after the declaration of war and the Intimate was the first London theatre to re-open with a production of Terence Rattigan's *French Without Tears*. Playgoers were advised that 'In the event of an air raid warning being sounded during the performance the fact will be announced from the stage. Patrons who live within five minutes' walking distance can, of course, return home if they wish but others are strongly recommended to remain in their seats. The performance will continue.' Despite war conditions and many shortages, one of which was of young male actors, the Intimate continued as usual and provided much welcome entertainment,. There were new plays and revivals — one of which, *Richard of Bordeaux*,

99   *Vivien Leigh with the cast of* Spring at Marino *in 1957*

100   Outward Bound *at the Intimate Theatre in 1967*

101   Salisbury House

celebrated the hundredth appearance on this stage of the well known
actor, John Clements, who had run the Intimate since 1935. Six weeks later,
however, his association ended. In September 1940 Ivor Novello's *Full House*
was staged but the bombing of London had begun and audience numbers
fell so drastically that the theatre closed on 16 September. It was re-opened
a year later with a production of *French for Love*. A red light on the left of
the stage indicated that an air raid warning had sounded and a green one
that it was now 'all clear'. Many actors had been called up to join the armed
forces so replacement men had to be found. In September 1941 Richard
Attenborough, a fifteen-year-old student at the Royal Academy of Dramatic
Art, had a role in Eugene O'Neill's play *Ah, Wilderness!*. Costumes were

102 & 103   New libraries at Ponders End (right) and and Ridge Avenue (below)

another problem as clothes and material were rationed so actors had to supply their own clothes for plays in modern dress. The theatre was well patronised from 1942, when the bombing ceased temporarily, and a wide repertoire of plays was enjoyed from classics such as *The Merchant of Venice* and *The Importance of Being Earnest* to contemporary murders and comedies.

104   This 1939 building at Arnos Grove accommodates the library and swimming pool

Noel Coward's *This Happy Breed* proved so popular in 1945 that it had to be repeated three weeks later.

The post-war years of the late 1940s was the golden age of this theatre before television made its impact on attendance, The range of plays was as wide as before, from *Othello* to comedies such as *George and Margaret* which in December 1946 became the first complete play to be televised live by the BBC; for this transmission the Intimate received £59. Theatrical productions were changing in the same way as films and Harold Pinter (under his stage name of David Baron) appeared as Cliff in the Intimate's production of John Osborne's ground-breaking *Look Back in Anger*. Unfortunately, throughout Britain audiences were enticed away from repertory theatre and cinemas by television and the bitterly cold winter of 1962/3 also discouraged attendance. Attempts were made to help this theatre survive by having bingo sessions, old time music hall, musicals and pantomimes but in 1968 the end of Council financial support was a death blow and the premises reverted to being a church hall. The only other live professional entertainments in the boroughs were the occasional performances at the Regal Edmonton of musicals such as Lionel Bart's *Oliver* and *Blitz*, pantomimes and concerts of classical music by the London Philharmonic Orchestra. There were open air productions in Pymmes Park from 1946 until vandalism forced closure. Amateur dramatics were, however, a leisure activity for many and drama and opera societies performed regularly throughout and after the war in Church House, Southgate and other halls including, from 1969, St Monica's.

After the war workers had more leisure. Working hours were reduced and the five-day week became the norm. Housewives acquired washing machines, refrigerators, vacuum cleaners and other aids which reduced the time spent on household chores so they too had more free hours. Many local societies, which had been forced to close during the war, re-opened and a wide range of activities became available including bowling, choral singing, angling, horse

*105 (right) Enfield
Football Club wins the
FA Amateur Cup in
1967*

*106 (below) Cricket at
the Walker Ground*

107   *Bush Hill Park Clubhouse, one of several golf clubs in the borough*

108   *A running track and pavilion were opened in 1953 at Enfield Playing Fields*

109   Indoor swimming pool in Southgate

110   Barrowell Green outdoor swimming pool

riding, and, from 1950, archery. Historic Salisbury House was purchased by Edmonton Council and opened in 1957 as an arts centre which was used by many groups. Ex-servicemen joined the British Legion or other such clubs. The first Darby and Joan clubs were formed for the elderly and retired who are called 'the old' in the publications of this period. They proved very popular and the number of similar organisations set up in the district increased regularly throughout the next twenty-five years.

Many opted to spend some of their leisure hours on improving their qualifications, skills and interests at evening classes. There was a wide range of subjects offered by the three Education Committees, from mathematics and modern languages to mountaineering, ballroom dancing, sports and music appreciation. Photography courses became very popular as more people bought cameras. DIY (do-it-yourself) practical courses were added to the more academic subjects as more men wanted to acquire the skills to decorate, adapt and maintain their homes. Women were encouraged by sewing classes to make clothes for themselves and their children, and articles entitled 'Home dressmaking for wise readers' were a regular feature of local newspapers. There was also a revived interest in gardening as bomb shelters were demolished in back gardens and flowers replaced the vegetables which had been grown during the war.

Libraries have always provided a free source of knowledge and reading material, another important leisure activity. Enfield libraries issued 598,423 books in 1952 and claimed 'People are reading more in spite of television'. Mobile libraries from 1948 provided a service to outlying areas and new branches were opened in Ponders End, Southgate and Ridge Avenue. From 1939 at Arnos Grove the library was housed in the same new building as the swimming pool.

However, a survey of young people in 1960 found that they were dissatisfied with the leisure facilities available and wanted bowling, dancing, music records and coffee bars which were not provided by youth clubs.

The Gazette announced the return of the television service in 1945 with the headline 'Television is here — all live' and reported on a broadcast from Bulls Cross Farm. By 1955 when the first commercial TV station opened, with an advert for Gibbs toothpaste, television had become the major leisure activity, a fact that was underlined when in 1960 *Radio Times* placed television programmes in the front pages with radio at the back. BBC Two was added as a third channel: its remit was 'to educate and entertain the British public' and it produced some classic series such as Kenneth Clark's *Civilisation*. From 1968 transmissions were available in colour.

Many people enjoyed sports as spectators or participants. With no professional football club in the boroughs fans travelled to Highbury or Tottenham to support Arsenal or Spurs. Arsenal's ground was requisitioned as an ARP post during the war and the two teams had to share the White Hart Lane ground. To save on travel, regional leagues were set up but games continued to attract supporters even though both teams had lost many players to the armed forces. Enfield Football Club continued to play throughout this period and celebrated winning the Football Association Amateur Cup in 1967 by touring the town in an open top bus, cheered by many supporters. Others enjoyed watching cricket at the Walker Ground, Southgate, which has attracted spectators for over 100 years, and rugby football at Saracens' ground

111   Enjoying the local countryside

112   Boating on a park lake

113   River Lea, popular with anglers

114   Bowling in a park

115   Model yachts on a local pond

in Southgate. Gymkhanas and point-to-point races were also popular in the 1950s and 20,000 horse lovers are said to have attended the races at Holly Hill Farm.

Facilities for those wishing to participate in sport were limited during the war because many playing fields were dug up as allotments or camps for prisoners of war had been built on them. However cricket was played on a

116 & 117   *Shopping in Palmers Green (above) and in Enfield Market (below)*

makeshift basis at the Paulin Ground, Winchmore Hill and by local clubs in Edmonton. When the war ended a wide range of sporting opportunities became available again and from 1947 tennis, putting and miniature golf were permitted on Sundays in local parks. Golf became more popular after the war and more clubs were opened as demand increased. A new running track at Enfield Playing Fields in 1953 improved the athletics facilities. Swimming also became a year round recreation with the opening of the indoor baths in Southgate in 1966 to supplement the open-air pools in Enfield and Winchmore Hill.

Restrictions on travel during the war years prevented most people from taking a holiday. The three councils provided 'Holidays at home' attractions with concerts, dances, sports and community singing which would include patriotic songs such as 'There'll always be an England' and anti-Nazi ones, 'We're going to hang out the washing on the Siegfried Line'. In the late 1940s some resorts and holiday camps re-opened and families were able to enjoy a seaside holiday again. This was also the time when the day trips were most popular as few had their own car so travel was by coach, train or boat. By the 1950s many could afford to travel further afield and the European continent had recovered to some extent from the German occupation. As air travel became cheaper, many ventured abroad for the first time — Spain, France and Austria were often the destination and in the 1960s holidays further afield, to Greece, Russia and Poland were advertised.

Because of the proximity of the countryside, walking and cycling were constant leisure activities, while many enjoyed boating on local lakes and rivers. The opening up of the green belt and the purchase of Forty Hall as a public park added considerably to the area available. Even more leisure facilities were being built and would open in the early 1970s. Some of these were being developed because in 1961 the Mayor of Hackney invited representatives from eighteen local authorities to a boat trip along the River Lea. His purpose was to emphasise the need for joint action to clean up the river and rescue the surrounding land from dereliction. The group found much to convince them of the scope for improving the area for the benefit and enjoyment of the people. As a result, an increase in sporting opportunities was assured when in 1962 plans were approved to develop recreation facilities on the banks of the River Lea from Hackney to Ware. Enfield was to have boating and canoeing centres near Enfield Lock and in 1969 £400,000 was paid for 73 acres of land at Picketts Lock, Edmonton, which was to be developed as a sports centre with a swimming pool, golf course and many other facilities.

There were also leisure activities for many other interests. The poetry writing group was no doubt encouraged in 1969 by the award of the Queen's Medal for Poetry to Palmers Green resident, Stevie Smith. Choral singing was favoured by many and there were concerts throughout the area. Bowling became popular, both indoors and in the parks, while others followed more specialist interests in archaeology, flower arranging, art, embroidery, brass rubbing, woodwork, bridge, model yachts and many other pursuits. In this chapter it has been possible to cover only the major leisure activities, to which should probably be added, from the 1960s onwards — shopping.

CHAPTER 6

Transport

'**I**s your journey really necessary?' were the words on posters which were widely displayed during World War II. All oil had to be imported and the aim was that as much of it as possible should be reserved for use by the armed forces for tanks, planes and other military vehicles. Trains, fuelled by coal, ran on the usual local routes, taking workers to Central London and non-essential travel such as pleasure trips was discouraged. Such was the importance of the railway network that the Government took control of it for the duration of the war. Trains were needed to convey troops around Britain, to deliver raw materials to the factories producing weapons, ammunition and vehicles, and then to take these products to the appropriate military bases. The line through Ponders End Station was at its busiest ever as most of the output from local munition factories was transported by rail. First class travel by train was suspended as a wartime economy measure and lights were extinguished and name plates removed at all stations. The roads were less busy as fuel oil was strictly rationed and only those for whose war work a car was essential

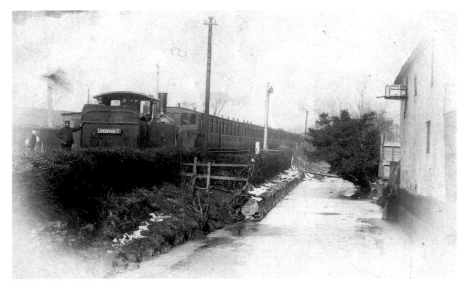

118   Edmonton Lower Level Station

119 *Diesel train at Winchmore Hill Station*

120 *Gordon Hill Station in the 1950s*

121 & 122   Building the new tunnel at Hadley Wood

123   Edmonton Junction looking south in 1961

124 Electrification of the Enfield Town line

125   *Escalators at Southgate Underground Station, now Grade II listed*

were allocated coupons. Most private cars were garaged for the duration of the war. Bus services were maintained during this difficult period. Measures were taken to prevent injury to passengers during an air raid, such as windows being covered with a mesh-like tape, interior lights dimmed and external lights hooded to prevent observation by enemy aircraft at night. Of course, there was no civil aviation. Pill boxes and tank barriers were constructed at stations such as Gordon Hill and Ponders End to impede enemy advances in the event of an invasion. The Churchbury Loop which had been closed to passenger traffic since 1919 was used as a diversionary route when the Lea Valley lines were blocked by engineering works or enemy action.

By 1945 the rail network was in poor shape; all services throughout Britain had been badly affected by enemy action with hundreds of railway vehicles and many properties damaged or destroyed, including the signal box at Brimsdown. When the war ended rail services in the Enfield area were again operated by the London North Eastern Railway until nationalisation in 1948, then becoming part of the Eastern Region of British Railways — the name was changed to British Rail in 1964. In almost every edition of the local papers from 1946 there were complaints about rail travel: the overcrowding, the necessity for a more frequent service, the need for electrification of the lines and a desire for the extension of the Underground network. Improvements came slowly. In 1955 British Railways announced a modernisation programme with electrification of some of the routes to Enfield and Edmonton and three years later trains formed of new diesel multiple units replaced the steam services

126 & 127   *Cockfosters Station (above) and the platforms (below)*

128   Old-type tube train used in 1930s and 1940s

on the Hertford North line, with stops at Palmers Green, Winchmore Hill, Grange Park, Enfield Chase, Gordon Hill and Crews Hill. Improvements to the signalling system on this line did not happen until 1972, while electrification was delayed until 1976. In 1959 Hadley Wood Station, on the main line from King's Cross to the north and Scotland, was rebuilt as a result of the much needed widening of the track and the construction of an additional tunnel. This line serves the most westerly area of the borough through New Southgate and Hadley Wood. When in 1960 the lines to Edmonton, Enfield Town and eastern Enfield on the Hertford East route were electrified, the rebuilding of many bridges and stations, including Enfield Town, and the installation of overhead power lines were essential. The Clapton to Cheshunt line, which served Edmonton and eastern Enfield, however was excluded from the scheme. The Churchbury Loop which had been closed to passengers for almost fifty years, was re-opened as the Southbury Loop, with Churchbury and Forty Hill stations renamed Southbury and Turkey Street. Gradually at all stations electric lights replaced gas lamps and the signal system was updated. With the phasing out of steam engines the large coal yards at many stations became redundant. British Rail made a loss of £87 million in 1951 and the Chairman was told by the Government to make a plan to turn this to a profit. The Beeching Report proposed the closing of almost half the rail network and a reduction in the workforce of 70,000. The main line services were to continue as were the commuter routes around London so local travel was not affected. However in other parts of Britain lines survived only if they could make the same amount of profit as the London area.

The Piccadilly Line of the London Underground system had only been

129   Metro Cammell train immobilised by snow at Oakwood

extended to Southgate, Oakwood (then called Enfield West) and Cockfosters in 1933 but had proved popular with commuters. The LPTB (London
Passenger Transport Board) planned well in advance for the possible effects
of bombing of the system. Their engineering department was reorganised
to deal with bomb damage and gas attacks and resources made available
for emergency repairs and the maintenance of train services. Emergency
communication equipment was installed with additional offices and control
rooms set up across the network in case some were destroyed by enemy action.
An ARP special unit was trained to deal with rescue arrangements. LPTB staff
formed two battalions of the Home Guard. All location signs were removed
and the windows of Piccadilly Line trains were blacked out as they ran above
ground at both ends of the line. Blast walls were built outside station entrances
and windows were covered with sticky tape to reduce the possibility of injury
from broken glass. The Underground trains played a part in the evacuation of
children, as convoys of some of the 200,000 London evacuees travelled on the
Piccadilly Line to Oakwood in 1939 on their way to the country.

When the Blitz on London began in 1940 many people believed that the
deep level Underground tube stations were safe places and sought shelter
on the platforms. However, the stations above ground, such as Arnos Grove,
Oakwood and Cockfosters, did not offer this protection so were not used
in this way. At Bounds Green, just outside the borough boundary, a bomb
exploded in the tunnel in October 1940 killing nineteen people who were
sheltering there. There was massive damage to the line and the Piccadilly Line
service had to be suspended for two months.

After the war there was increased traffic on the northern section of the

130   RT2978 bus at the terminus, The Goat, Forty Hill

Piccadilly Line as housing developments took place in the Southgate, Oak-wood and Cockfosters areas. By 1951 millions of passengers per year were using Cockfosters station, fifteen extra trains a day were added to the service and gradually the old ones were replaced by a new type. The Metro Cammell 'silver' trains with their fluorescent lighting and modern features entered service in September 1957. London Transport had announced in 1952 that they would increase passenger capacity by 15 per cent. However complaints continued to appear in the press regularly and the *Palmers Green & Southgate Gazette* called the service 'disgraceful' in October 1959. The first major improvement to local transport came with the opening of the Victoria Line in 1968 when access to the West End of London and main line stations became easier with interchanges with rail services at Seven Sisters, Tottenham Hale and Finsbury Park.

    Like the trains and the Underground, local bus services played a role in the evacuation programme of 1939, shuttling people between pick up points to railway stations or taking them all the way to their destinations. Most bus and coach services at this time were operated by the LPTB with garages in Ponders End, Palmers Green and Edmonton. The advent of the war resulted in the running down of bus manufacturing and LPTB had to supplement its ageing fleet with ad-hoc vehicles. It also had to abandon its high engineering design standard and purchase vehicles known as 'Utility' buses. The 'Guy' type of such buses was used in the Enfield area on several routes including 107/107A from Enfield Lock and 121 from Ponders End, all painted in drab brown livery. After the war the most common type of vehicle became the red double-decker RT class bus until it was replaced by the Routemaster in 1969.

    Trolleybuses had replaced trams in 1938 and ran, at first, along four main

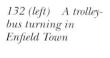

131 (above)   The coming of the trolleybus

132 (left)   A trolley-bus turning in Enfield Town

133 (left)   A trolley-bus on route 629

134.   A Routemaster bus and remnants of old trolleybus wiring

135   Floods at Silver Street, Edmonton, brought traffic to a halt

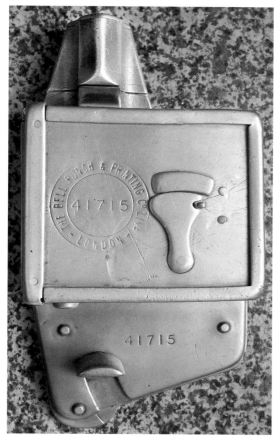

136 & 137 (above)   Bell punch and its ticket

138 & 139 Below)   Gibson ticket-issuing machine and its ticket

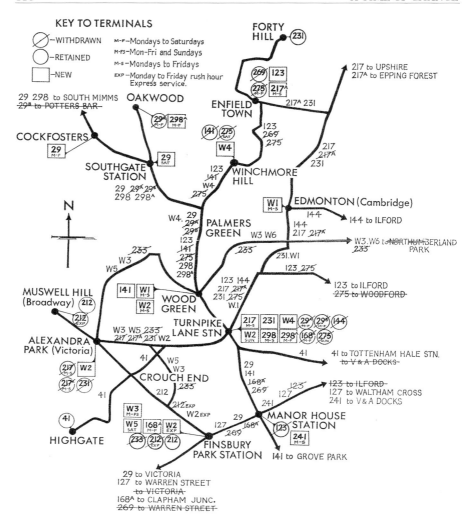

KEY TO TERMINALS

⊘ —WITHDRAWN   M-F—Mondays to Saturdays
◯ —RETAINED   M-FS—Mon-Fri and Sundays
▢ —NEW   M-S—Mondays to Fridays
                EXP—Monday to Friday rush hour
                    Express service.

140   New bus services from September 1968

routes from Waltham Cross: 627 to Tottenham Court Road, 649 to Liverpool Street Station, 659 to Holborn Circus and 679 to Smithfield. Other trolleybuses ran on route 629 from Enfield Town to Tottenham Court Road and route 641 from Winchmore Hill to Moorgate. Most trolleybus services operated until 1961 when, under 'Stage 10 of the Trolleybus Conversion Plan', they were replaced by Routemasters. The removal of overhead wiring resulted in the potential to have greater flexibility but the increase in road traffic negated this to some extent and traffic congestion did not decline. The method of issuing tickets also changed. Until the 1950s the bell-punch punched a ticket with the appropriate valid stage fare but it was replaced by the Gibson ticket-issuing machine, which printed the fare and fare stage on a roll of paper.

After the war there were shortages and petrol rationing. Public transport played a significant part in daily life but, as described in Chapter 2 on the years of austerity, the standard of living began to rise: there was virtual full employment and consequent staff shortages on the buses which impacted on the reliability of public transport. Staff vacancies from London Transport, which had replaced the LPTB, appeared in the local papers every week and their recruitment campaigns brought many workers from the Caribbean to fill the vacancies for drivers and conductors. By the mid-1950s industrial unrest started to appear and this culminated in the seven-week bus strike from 5 May 1958. This, together with greater prosperity, encouraged a move away from bus travel to private cars.

In 1966 London Transport published a report 'Reshaping of London's Bus Services' which in essence put forward a plan to combat the two main problems of operation, traffic congestion and staff shortages. This envisaged more 'one man operated' single-deck buses acting as flat fare feeder services and the introduction of new methods of fare collection. These were eventually introduced on 7 September 1968 and resulted in many services being re-routed and new routes introduced in the Enfield area.

There was some modification to the routes of London Country Buses during the war but afterwards they resumed services on three routes in the

141   *Barges on the River Lea*

142   A zebra crossing in Enfield Town

Enfield area, all terminating in Cecil Road, Enfield Town. Route 313 to St Albans was extended during the summer periods to Whipsnade Zoo: the 310 served Hertford while the 310A terminated at Rye House. Greenline services were suspended during the war but from 1946 provided a long distance link. The 715 from Hertford to Guildford was routed via Enfield Town while the 715A went via Ponders End and Edmonton and terminated at Marble Arch. In 1962 to increase capacity the coaches were replaced by double-decker buses.

Before the boom in car ownership there was a period just after the war when people enjoyed excursions by public transport to places such as London Airport, Windsor, Chessington Zoo and Hampton Court. In addition to London Transport, private companies, such as George Ewer's Grey Green Coaches ran a programme of excursions from one of its premises in Edmonton and provided coach travel to holiday destinations. Empire's Best ran a regular all year round service from London to Clacton via Palmers Green and Enfield. This service consisted of three trips each way daily.

Transportation by water declined throughout the period. During the war some coal to Brimsdown Power Station was conveyed by barges on the River Lea, as were some of the raw materials used by the Royal Small Arms Factory and other weapons manufacturers. In 1947 all British waterways were nationalised and placed under the control of the British Transport Commission. As leisure time and facilities increased, canoes, rowing boats, decorated barges and other pleasure craft soon outnumbered working vessels.

The biggest change in transportation in the thirty years covered in this book was the increase in car ownership which resulted in much heavier traffic on the roads. Before the war few families owned cars but by 1950 there were 2.3 million on British roads. One result of the increased traffic was a rise in the number of accidents, especially to pedestrians and cyclists, and so the Government organised a campaign 'Keep Death off the Roads'. By 1964 the number of vehicles had risen to over nine million and every edition of the local newspapers contained adverts for Hillman, Austin, Morris, Vauxhall and other British-manufactured cars. The Suez crisis of 1956 created a shortage of petrol and an increase in its cost: this contributed to the success of the Mini, an icon of the 1950s, which used less fuel than other models.

Changes were introduced to deal with the problems created by the increase in traffic; car parks were built, such as the one at the Triangle, Palmers Green which was little used at first even though it was free of charge. Many motorists continued to park in the street and in 1950 the Southgate police actually appealed to drivers to use the car parks. As persuasion proved unsuccessful the first 'yellow bands', as yellow lines were then called, appeared on main roads and bus routes to indicate where parking was prohibited or restricted. Parking meters in some places followed in 1958 and traffic wardens in 1960. In 1965 the Minister of Transport, Mrs Barbara Castle, introduced the breathalyser to test the amount of alcohol consumed by drivers. This was one of the measures designed to reduce accidents together with a 70mph maximum speed limit, seat belts and zebra crossings. All contributed to a reduction in the death rate from road accidents. Less noteworthy was the 1969 'Big Road Scheme' to make the North Circular Road dual carriageway at The Cock, Palmers Green as this was not achieved until the twenty-first century.

By 1968 there were 50,000 cars in the London Borough of Enfield and subways were built under the Great Cambridge Road for pedestrians. The defeat of the Council's proposal for a ring road through St Andrew's graveyard, the Grammar School grounds and Holly Walk is described in Chapter 10 'Enfield Preservation Society'. Instead a one-way gyratory system was introduced in Enfield Town and worked well. In the following years the number of vehicles on the roads continued to increase, encouraged to some extent, by the creation of a network of motorways.

CHAPTER 7

Health

Information in the reports of the MOHs (Medical Officers of Health) during World War II was limited by a directive from the Ministry of Health which, on the grounds of national security, ordered that nothing should be included, such as statistics of casualties and deaths from enemy action, which could be used as propaganda by the enemy. Each of the annual reports for 1939-45 is, therefore, brief. When war threatened, the efforts of the Public Health Departments were concentrated at first in building up an efficient ARP casualty service so many buildings, such as Enfield's maternity and child welfare clinics and Broomfield House, were converted into emergency first aid posts. The Public Health Departments were also made responsible for the management of the nurseries which were established throughout the three boroughs to care for pre-school children while their mothers worked. The Medical Officers expressed concern at the outbreak of war about shortages of staff because doctors, nurses and other medical personnel had joined the armed services and also about the adequacy of hospital accommodation to cope with the expected number of casualties. MOH Edmonton wrote in his 1939 report: 'Unfortunately ARP activities, consequent on the declaration of war, brought the whole of the medical services to a standstill for three weeks, and then ordinary service resumed'. He also noted that four nurses had been transferred to areas where local children had been evacuated. All MOHs' reports during the war years stated that the general health of the population was good and nutrition satisfactory. The main cause of death throughout the war was given as coronary diseases in Edmonton, Enfield and Southgate. Measles epidemics, which occurred regularly every two years, and outbreaks of scabies were common concerns to all of them. Efforts were made to prevent the spread of diseases and germs by Government campaigns. One poster which was displayed on public transport was 'Trap those germs in your handkerchief and help to keep the nation fighting fit'.

During the war the hospitals, whether municipal or voluntary aided, were brought together into a single emergency medical service. Chase Farm was an old people's home until 1939 when it was adapted to deal with war casualties. Dr Allan Birch in his 'Brief History of Chase Farm Hospital', published in the *Enfield Medical Gazette,* No 1, 1969, recalled that the Medical Director 'faced the great task of making the buildings function as a hospital'. There was no equipment so 50-gallon water tanks were converted into sterilisers, biscuit tins into dressing drums and cow troughs into bed-pan washers. The hospital was functioning completely ten weeks after the start of the war and was very busy when the Blitz on London began the following year: one bombing

143 *Aerial View of Chase Farm Hospital*

144   *The South Wing of North Middlesex Hospital, Edmonton*

incident resulted in the staff dealing with 350 casualties in three days. When the Whitechapel victims of the Blitz on the East End arrived at the hospital, nurses found shards of glass and pieces of rubble in their clothes and hair. In addition to the civilian casualties, service men and women were admitted, including German prisoners of war, allied troops, such as Polish airmen and Free French fighters, as well as British personnel. Despite the pressure of work some doctors and nurses played a part in the Dig for Victory campaign by growing vegetables on allotments in the hospital grounds. A former nurse at Chase Farm Hospital, Mrs P. Bloomfield, wrote in *The Nurse's Story* that when the naval gun on Slades Hill was in action the main doors of the hospital were blasted open and that during daytime air raids, nurses, who had been on night duty had to sleep on mattresses in the corridors. All staff were trained to evacuate patients in an emergency. The patients were lifted on to the floor on their mattresses and then ropes were brought across to secure them before they were taken on a bumpy ride down the stairs. When the war ended Chase Farm became a general hospital serving the Enfield area and a school of nursing was established.

The other major hospital in the district, the North Middlesex in Edmonton, had opened in 1910 but had shared the site with the workhouse until this was closed in 1938. Plans had been drawn up to extend the hospital into the buildings vacated by the workhouse but some were considered unfit for hospital use and were demolished. When war was declared the re-building plans had to be shelved. During the war the hospital received two direct hits

145   Bomb damage to the North Middlesex Hospital

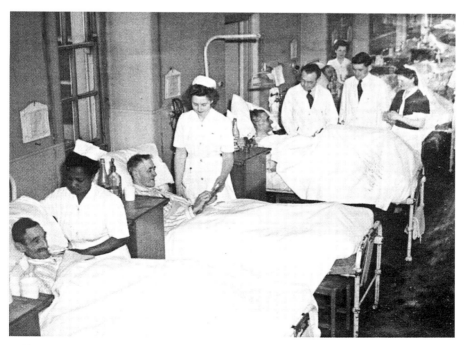

146   Doctors and nurses at the North Middlesex Hospital in the 1950s

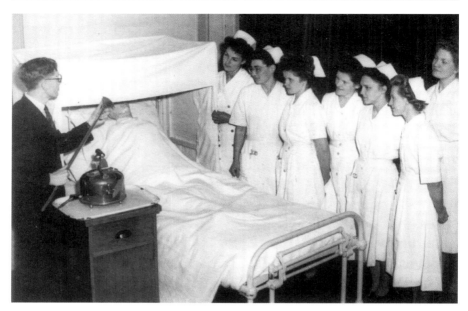

147   A ward at the North Middlesex Hospital in the 1950s

and suffered further damage from another two bombs which landed close by. First, an incendiary device fell in September1940 and damaged the west wing and the chapel but there was no loss of life. Then in December 1940, a parachute mine, which fell nearby, further damaged the hospital, and in April 1944 six bombs, thought to be some of the last to be dropped in the area by a piloted aircraft, fell within a radius of 100 yards in the hospital grounds and resulted in the loss of 350 beds and the destruction of the orthopaedic, casualty, fracture, reception and x-ray departments. Nine patients, five staff and two St John Ambulance men were killed. The final damage occurred in March 1945 when a V2 rocket fell in nearby Wilbury Way and shattered the windows of the hospital. After the war the hospital continued to operate and the bombed buildings were gradually rebuilt.

The Northern Hospital (its name was changed to Highlands in 1948) until the outbreak of war was a specialised unit engaged in the treatment of infectious diseases, especially tuberculosis and encephalitis. In 1939 its role was extended to include an emergency bed service under the aegis of the London Hospital. Medical and surgical cases were transferred twice weekly from hospitals in the East End. The staff was increased by the arrival of medical students, nurses and doctors from the London Hospital and others which had been forced by the bombing to close wards. So the Northern became a general hospital for the first time but treated no local residents, only cases brought in from other areas. The Northern Regional Centre for the treatment and rehabilitation of traumatic and orthopaedic cases was added to the medical services available in 1942. By 1945 the 800 beds were allocated as: 300 for encephalitis, 100 for TB, 100 for traumatic and orthopaedic surgery and 300 for emergency cases,

148   Highlands Hospital

149.   Grovelands Hospital, Southgate

150   St Michael's Hospital

151   War Memorial Cottage Hospital, Enfield

152   White Lodge Surgery, Silver Street, Enfield

including members of the armed services. When the war ended there was a
decline in the workload and the role of the hospital was changed to that of a
general hospital, serving the residents of Southgate and Winchmore Hill. In
1966 it merged with South Lodge, a neighbouring hospital, and the 500 beds
were divided into 160 medical and surgical, forty geriatric, sixty orthopaedic,
twenty-five gynaecology, fifteen children, sixty encephalitis, thirty ear, nose
and throat, twelve TB, twelve isolation and smaller numbers for maternity,
diseases of the chest and intensive care. A nurse training school functioned
until 1969.

There were several smaller hospitals in the district. Grovelands
Hospital, Southgate, was used by the Royal Northern Hospital Group for
patient treatment and convalescence during the war and continued as a
convalescent home until taken over by the National Health Service (NHS)
in 1948. Local GPs could treat their own patients at the small War Memorial
Hospital in Enfield. There were only three wards, an operating theatre and
an outpatients department. Like St Michael's Hospital it became a satellite
of Chase Farm.

Until the arrival of the NHS, doctors charged fees for each surgery
or home visit. Some people had private health insurance but the elderly,
housewives and children were excluded from such schemes and so they, and
the uninsured, had to pay. There was no appointment system and patients

First get a recommendation from your family doctor that your eyes need testing. Then hand that recommendation to any doctor with special qualifications (lists will be available) or to any ophthalmic optician taking part in the new service. If you need glasses, these will be provided without charge. For re-testing you can go direct to any of the doctors with special qualifications, or to an ophthalmic optician.

The National Health Service will provide several kinds of spectacles of different types. For specially expensive types you will have to pay the extra cost.

Deafness Specialist ear clinics will be established as resources allow. At them you will get not only an expert opinion upon deafness but also, if necessary, a *new hearing aid* invented by a special committee of the Medical Research Council. Production of these aids is now going on, but will not meet all demands at once. They will be supplied free, when ready, together with a reasonable allowance of maintenance batteries.

Home Health Services Your local County or County Borough Council will, as soon as it can, make special provision for: (1) advice and care of expectant and nursing mothers and children under five (for particulars ask your doctor, health visitor, or Welfare Centre); (2) midwifery (ask your doctor or Welfare Centre); (3) home nursing where there is illness in the family (ask your doctor); (4) all necessary vaccination or immunisation (through your doctor or Welfare Centre); and (5) a health visitor service to deal with problems of illness in the home, especially tuberculosis.

Health Centres Special premises known as Health Centres may later be opened in your district. Doctors may be accommodated there instead of in their own surgeries, but you will still have "your own doctor" to give you personal and confidential treatment. He will still come to your home as necessary. At the Health Centre he will be able to use equipment supplied from public funds. These Centres may also offer dentistry and other services on the spot.

WHAT TO DO NOW

1. Choose your doctor.
2. Get application forms from him or from the Post Office, Public Library, or office of the local Executive Council.
3. Fill one in for each member of the family.
4. Hand them to the doctor.

ACT AT ONCE

PREPARED BY THE CENTRAL OFFICE OF INFORMATION FOR THE MINISTRY OF HEALTH

(KBE7.7) Wt. 20103 2/48 Hw.

THE NEW

NATIONAL HEALTH SERVICE

Your new National Health Service begins on 5th July. What is it? How do you get it?

It will provide you with all medical, dental, and nursing care. Everyone—rich or poor, man, woman or child—can use it or any part of it. There are no charges, except for a few special items. There are no insurance qualifications. But it is not a "charity". You are all paying for it, mainly as taxpayers, and it will relieve your money worries in time of illness.

153 *National Health Service leaflet*

were seen on a first come, first served basis. At White Lodge Surgery in Silver Street, Enfield, people waited on rows of highly polished benches along which they slid as they moved closer to the front. Doctors made up their own prescriptions. In the *History of White Lodge Surgery* Kenneth Rainbird recalled:

> When I was a child the surgery made up its own prescriptions which the patients collected later in the day. During the war, when I was 11 or 12, I was lucky enough to be hired to deliver the prescriptions to various parts of Enfield. I think I took the place of a gentleman who had joined the army. It covered quite a large area and I was provided with a White Lodge delivery bike with a carrier and basket in the front filled with bottles and boxes which I had collected from the pharmacy in White Lodge.

With the success of the Labour Party in the 1945 election the creation of a national health service was assured. Many doctors had doubts about the change and that year the British Medical Association, at a meeting of doctors at the North Middlesex Hospital, called for action to keep health services 'out of the control of politicians'. The MOHs reported that the health of many of the working class in 1945 was better than pre-war as their diet had more nutritional value. Rationing was partly responsible as it had led to a fair allocation of all that was available and also a diet which had contained plenty of fresh fruit and vegetables. Children's teeth were better because sweet rationing allowed them just one bar of chocolate or its equivalent per

154   *De Bohun Health Clinic, Southgate*

week. However 'diphtheria more deadly than the bombs' was still prevalent in the 1940s and parents were constantly reminded in the local press to get their children immunised.

In 1946 the MOHs complained that an increasing and varied number of social services available to the population had put an additional burden on the shoulders of the local public health authority staff, as they were now responsible for schemes such as Home Help and Domestic Help. They all stressed that poor housing was still a major factor affecting health and urged a speedy replacement of the slum areas.

The first case of polio was reported in Edmonton in 1947. This soon became an epidemic with eighteen cases. All the boroughs had cases for a further thirteen years and swimming pools were closed as a possible source of infection. Another concern in Enfield at this time was the condition of the New River Loop which Enfield's MOH reported was a health hazard, full of dumped rubbish and polluted by weeds and fallen leaves. Southgate MOH's concern was the average diet, which he said was worse than during the war as current rations of 2,700 calories a day were the minimum needed to control disease and maintain health.

In July 1948 the National Health Service became a reality. A leaflet entitled 'The New National Health Service' was sent to every home. It stated that the NHS 'will provide you with all medical, dental and nursing care. Everyone, rich or poor, man, woman or child can use any part of it'. Every person had to register at a local doctor's surgery. Some lists were soon fully subscribed as the maximum number of patients allowed per doctor was 4,000. In the first weeks a flood of people went to surgeries, hospitals, health clinics, pharmacies, opticians and dentists to benefit

155 Princess Margaret opens the new Outpatients Department at North Middlesex Hospital in 1960

from the National Health Service 'free at the point of use'. GPs (general practitioners) had negotiated an agreement whereby their salary would be based on the number of patients they treated rather than a flat yearly sum and they were also permitted to continue to treat patients privately. Some doctors expressed concern that they were being called to patients' homes for house visits for cases which should have been brought to their surgeries. They no longer made up their own medicines but gave patients a written prescription to take to a pharmacy.

In the late 1940s the birth rate rose to record levels in all three boroughs: quads were born at the North Middlesex Hospital. Southgate's isolation hospital in Tottenhall Road became a maternity unit to increase the number of beds. MCC (Middlesex County Council) took over responsibility for maternity and child services from the boroughs' health officers. Cases of diphtheria declined – there were none in Southgate by 1947 but there was a 123 per cent increase in personal accidents both in the home and to pedestrians and cyclists. An increase in TB was thought to be due in part to 'war conditions which of necessity led to the spread of diseases and low resistance to infection'. The 1949 reports contain mentions of environmental health for the first time and health education featured prominently in Edmonton's

156   Rebuilding work at the North Middlesex Hospital

annual report. There is, also, universal concern about the soaring cost of the
Health Service.

A shortage of maternity beds continued into the next decade as in 1950
the highest birth rate ever was recorded. Parents were worried about polio
and Southgate's MOH advised them not to let their children paddle in lakes
or ponds as a precaution. He described Southgate as 'A healthy borough
but there is difficulty in getting hospital admission for the chronic sick and
elderly'. Food poisoning was not mentioned in the health statistics of the
1940s but is included in the annual reports of the 1950s after the Government
introduced legislation about food hygiene which was added to the local
MOHs' responsibilities. The *Palmers Green Gazette* advised 'Do you want to be
poisoned? Keep away from fly-infested cafés'. However it was the 275 cases
of food poisoning at Minchenden School which accounted for much of that
year's statistic in Southgate.

In 1951 the birth rate began to decline. There was a mild flu epidemic but
the general health of the public was judged to be better than ever. However,
there was a continued shortage of beds for the elderly: St Michael's Hospital
was turning people away and geriatric units were set up. The three main
problems at this time were identified as TB, mental illness and old age. Polio
remained a major concern until 1953 with sixteen cases (including one death)

157   *Helicopter air ambulance in Hertford Road*

in Enfield. There were fewer cases of diphtheria and scarlet fever in 1952 but an increasing number of patients were suffering from intestinal complaints, allergies and chronic neurosis. The clearance of the slums and the building of new homes had improved the living conditions of many but there was still much to do. In 1954 hospital costs rose to £17 a week per patient as the expenditure of the NHS continued to soar.

The following year a considerable increase in deaths from lung cancer was highlighted and this was attributed to smoking. MOHs suggested that smoking should be banned in cinemas and other places of entertainment and from August 1965 advertisements for cigarettes were banned from television. Diphtheria disappeared from the reports and the number of new cases of polio declined as the Salk vaccine was developed. Vaccination against polio was offered to children and later to fifteen to twenty-five year olds. Mobile x-ray units on the streets led to earlier identification and treatment of TB and a consequent reduction in deaths. However, Enfield's road accident rate was shown to be higher than the national average.

The first family planning clinics opened in the late 1950s. They were so well used that there was a demand for more of them with longer opening hours, particularly when the contraceptive pill became available. An Asian flu epidemic put pressure on beds in local hospitals at a time when they were short of staff. There were also the first cases of the thalidomide drug disaster. The drug had been prescribed to pregnant women and was responsible for a large number of badly deformed children, some with missing limbs.

By the end of the decade smoke control had been enforced in all the boroughs and the air was less polluted.

Princess Margaret visited the North Middlesex Hospital in 1960 to open the new Outpatients Department, built to replace the one destroyed in the bombing. A £3.25 million face lift for this hospital was announced in December 1967 and building began in the late 1960s.

A few cases of smallpox, which was considered to have been eradicated in Britain, in Tottenham in 1962 led many Edmonton residents to seek vaccination and no cases occurred in the neighbouring borough.

The reports of the 1960s showed a marked increase in cases of lung cancer. By 1965 deaths from cancer almost equalled the number from coronary disease. Alarm was expressed at the number of schoolchildren smoking in Edmonton and Southgate. On the positive side for the first time in thirteen years MOH Enfield reported no cases of polio. He urged parents not to be complacent about diphtheria but to continue to have their children vaccinated. He blamed the increase in lung cancer on the 'Brilliant advertising of the tobacco manufacturers'. Outbreaks of food poisoning and the very cold and foggy weather affected the young and the old and there was a rise in hospital admissions.

From mid-1965, with the amalgamation of Edmonton, Enfield and Southgate into the London Borough of Enfield (LBE) there was only one Medical Officer of Health and consequently only one yearly report, instead of three. Edmonton's former Medical Officer was selected for the post and his first report for the new borough records that the major cause of death remained coronary disease. TB deaths had fallen to seven and there were no cases of polio. The 'strain of modern life' was mentioned and a ten-year health plan for the LBE included more mental health centres. In addition to the health responsibilities of the three former boroughs, LBE now also took over those sections of public health which previously had been administered by the abolished Middlesex County Council.

There are some 'firsts' in the early reports on the health of LBE: problem families, screening for cancer of the cervix, and the use of an air ambulance helicopter to convey a patient to hospital. TB and road accident rates were down — the latter due to some degree to the introduction of the breathalyser. There was, however, a greater demand for psychiatric treatment and a recuperative hostel for the rehabilitation of psychiatric patients was opened in Windmill Hill. There was national publicity about drug dependency but the Medical Officer decided that this was not 'A problem of any magnitude' in the Borough of Enfield.

During the period covered by this chapter there were huge advances in medical research and treatment from which local people benefited: the first kidney dialysis machine was invented in 1944, hearing aids in 1956 and pacemakers in 1958. Charges had to be introduced, initially for spectacles and dental treatment, as the cost of the NHS spiralled but it remains one of the major achievements of these thirty years.

CHAPTER 8

EDUCATION

S chools did not re-open as scheduled after the summer holidays in September 1939 as war had been declared and thousands of children and some teachers were evacuated from Edmonton and Eastern Enfield. Schools had been prepared for a possible evacuation from these two areas which were considered to be most in danger of attack. Teachers were recalled by a message on the radio on 28 August to Houndsfield School for 'a complete rehearsal for evacuation: helpers, teachers, luggage, food, etc.'

158   *Pupils from Latymer School, Edmonton, were evacuated to Tonypandy, Wales, in 1940*

159   Enfield County School

On 1 September trolleybuses took the children from this school and from Raynham Road School to Lower Edmonton station for their onward journey by train to Braintree, Essex. Fifty staff and 457 pupils were also evacuated from the Latymer School before the war started. They were taken by train to Clacton-on-Sea where they shared the buildings of Clacton High School on a shift system: Clacton pupils used the classrooms in the morning and Latymer ones in the afternoon. When the expected blitz on London did not happen that year, many children returned home but there was nowhere for many of them to continue their schooling as their schools were closed so, after an interval, Latymer, Silver Street and a few other schools re-opened. There was a second stage of evacuation when the so-called 'phoney war' ended in May 1940 and the Blitz on London began. A hundred Latymer pupils and their siblings went to Cornwall with seven members of staff and those in Clacton were transferred to Tonypandy in the Rhondda Valley in South Wales because it was feared that the Nazi occupation of France, Belgium and the Netherlands would result in attacks on East Anglia. Most evacuees were billeted on families to whom the Government paid 10s 6d (52p) a week for the board and lodging of one child, and 17s (85p) for two.

The Government ordered that no school would be permitted to re-open until adequate provision against air raids had been provided so only some of the children in the so-called 'safer districts' of Enfield and Southgate who had not been offered the choice of evacuation, could return to their schools in October 1939. The boys of Chase Side School, Enfield, had a longer than expected holiday because the shelter at their school was not completed until January 1940. Similarly at Minchenden School, Southgate, the students were given assignments to take home until their shelter was built. Then pupils from Trinity County School, Wood Green, whose building had been requisitioned, joined them for the duration of the war together with some boys and girls from other schools which remained closed. The new first formers of Enfield County School met in groups in parents' houses while the more senior students went into the school briefly to hand in completed assignments and collect new ones. When their air-raid shelters were ready for use in the spring of 1940 the number of students at this school increased by about 40 per cent to 1,000 girls. Among them were 250 girls who had chosen not to be evacuated from Tottenham and Edmonton; they called themselves 'the left behinds.' It is recalled in the History of the Latymer School that the first forms soon got used to spending a large part of their time in the corridors of the North Block and in concrete shelters outside. The fifth and sixth forms, who had to take School Certificate, Matriculation and Higher School Certificate exams, also became accustomed to the aerial attacks and spent much of the time on the floor beneath their examination desks in the Great Hall. Other schools had to accommodate additional pupils. Keble Preparatory School in Winchmore Hill was requisitioned as a first aid post and so the boys joined the girls of Palmers Green High School. Some children were evacuated by private arrangements to friends or family in the country, and this so reduced the number of girls at St Angela's Convent that both the junior and senior schools were amalgamated on their site in Palmers Green.

Children were encouraged to play a part in the war effort. Parties of senior pupils from Enfield County and the Latymer Schools spent part of their summer holidays working on farms. An Enfield County girl wrote the following about the harvest camp in Suffolk in 1944: 'We camped under canvas in a field by the rectory. Miss F. Sharp organised the event and ran it like a regimental sergeant major! Other staff came for a week or more and they did all the donkey work in camp. But girls were allocated to help — even on latrine duty'. Girls knitted scarves, socks, mittens, gloves and balaclavas for the troops. Edmonton County pupils had been evacuated to Braintree and in one of their magazines it is reported that 'a frequent sight during the first weeks of term was that of girls walking along, busily knitting school jumpers. Having completed their own, they knitted more for refugees and people who had lost everything when their homes were bombed'. The Minchenden girls knitted items for the men in the armed forces and collected clothes for victims of the air raids while the boys' activities, as at Enfield Grammar School, included training with the ATC (Air Training Corps). Schools also joined enthusiastically in fund-raising efforts such as Wings for Victory and Salute the Soldier campaigns.

Schools attempted to continue lessons in the shelters during raids but it was crowded and difficult, one teacher complained that 'the atmosphere and heat were overpowering' which was the reason for the rush to 'bag' the benches near the door when the warning sounded. Some shelters did not have electricity and were lit by candles. In 1941 it was made compulsory for teachers to act as fire wardens on school premises. Rotas were set up to cover the night watches and training given on the use of stirrup pumps to extinguish fires caused by incendiary bombs. This proved useful when two such devices fell on Minchenden School. Later in 1941 a time bomb fell

160 & 161   Enfield County School gym was bombed so gymnastics and keep fit classes were held outdoors

162   One of the first secondary modern schools to be built was Chace Boys School, Enfield

on the hard courts of that school, which had to be evacuated for ten days until the Bomb Disposal Unit had removed the fuse from the unexploded bomb. Enfield County School also received a direct hit that year and the gym, tuckshop and two of the shelters were destroyed and all the windows blown out.

Because so many women worked during the war years there was a substantial increase in the number of nursery schools set up to care for children under five years of age. Houndsfield School was one of the places where nursery classes were introduced. Another consequence of the wartime conditions was that from 1940 school dinners were served for the first time: in Edmonton the cost was four pence (2p) per meal.

Although 1944 was the year of the V1 rocket attacks and the D-Day landings, the war time coalition government, with Winston Churchill as Prime Minister and Rab Butler as Minister of Education, passed the Education Act which came into force on 1 April 1945. Among the changes it introduced was the concentration of education powers in the hands of the county councils such as Middlesex, but some large districts, including Enfield, were granted a degree of autonomy. The most significant change was the separation of primary and secondary education. Before the 1944 Act, the school leaving age was fourteen and the majority of young people left school and started work at that age. The exceptions were those in private schools and those who had been successful in the Eleven Plus exams and could continue their education in grammar schools, although some refused such places because their

163   *School dinners at Oakwood Secondary Modern School*

164   *Cookery lessons at Oakwood Secondary Modern School in 1950*

165   Minchenden Lower School in Fox Lane

166   Forty Hill Primary School

167   *The new Walker Primary School, Southgate*

parents could not afford to pay for uniform and books. Secondary education for all was guaranteed, free of charge, in a grammar, secondary modern or technical school, from the age of 11. However an exam at this age continued to be held as the tool to select which children went where and those with the highest marks continued to enter the grammar schools. Secondary Moderns were a new type of school for the rest who previously would have remained in the senior forms of elementary schools until they were 14. The changes necessitated a large building programme and many new schools were needed but building materials were in short supply. Old schools needed repair as, like houses, maintenance had been neglected during the war. Miss M. C. Sharp, Headmistress of Enfield County School, spoke at the 1946 speech day of the 'slum like condition' of her school.

In 1946 local education committees had to draw up plans to bring schools into line with the new act. Southgate planned four new secondary schools, the re-building of one primary and the re-siting of the technical college. Edmonton needed seven new secondary schools. The first secondary moderns were, by necessity, opened in the classrooms which had been the senior departments of elementary schools until new purpose-built schools were ready; one of the first with new buildings was Chace Boys in 1956. An MCC

*168 & 169   New building and location for St Paul's C of E Primary School, Winchmore Hill,
which was opened by Princess Alexandra*

170   Enfield Collegiate School was one of the private schools which closed

leaflet was sent to parents to explain the new system of education: it stated 'schools would be organised and equipped in such a way as to offer an equal opportunity to all children according to their ability and so to give them the chance of achieving the highest degree of individual development of which they are capable and of finding their happier place in the world'. This led to a change of school for many children as primary classes were transferred to other schools so the buildings could be used as secondary moderns. As an example, the primary schoolchildren at Oakwood School were moved to Eversley School so that their Chase Road site could be developed as a secondary school. Southgate County School, which had outgrown its 1910 site, moved to Sussex Way, Cockfosters in 1960. Its Fox Lane premises were then used to accommodate the lower forms of Minchenden School and so ease the pressure on space at there. In the 1950s there was a shortage of space in most secondary schools as more children were encouraged to stay at school to sixteen and the school-leaving age had been raised to fifteen in 1947. HORSA (huts on raising school age) were erected at some schools to cope with the additional numbers — the four huts at Houndsfield School, Edmonton were erected with the help of German prisoners-of-war.

'Doubled birth rate brings school crisis' was the headline in the *Enfield Herald* of May 1950 which highlighted the shortfall of primary schools places as the children born in the record birth rate years of the 1940s reached five. New primary schools were built in Southgate and in areas such as Cuckoo

Trent Park Training College, Cockfosters.   PN5496.

171 & 172   Trent Park Teacher
Training College where Princess
Margaret was an early visitor

Hall, Carterhatch and Grange Park where there were housing developments
in the 1950s. St Paul's Church of England Primary School in Winchmore
Hill was re-built on a new site and opened by Princess Alexandra. Several
private schools did not survive the war or the difficult years which followed:
the Collegiate School, Winchmore Hill and Enfield Collegiate School were
among those which closed. Others stayed open throughout the war and the
following period. Palmers Green High School was one of these and in 1955

173 *Minchenden School*

174 *Southgate College's new building*

175   *Capel Manor*

celebrated its Golden Jubilee with a service at which memories of the school in its early years, written by former pupil, Stevie Smith, the well known poet and Palmers Green resident, were read by another famous 'old girl', the actress Dame Flora Robson.

There were shortages of teachers at both primary and secondary levels. To help with this, emergency teacher training colleges were set up all over Britain and it was proposed that Trent Park should be used for this purpose. At first some MCC councillors opposed this plan as they wanted the mansion to become a children's home, but in 1947 the first 210 students, mostly married men who had recently been 'demobbed' from the armed services, began their training to become teachers. Princess Margaret was one of the early visitors to the college.

The old School Certificate and Higher School Certificate were replaced in 1951 by the General Certificate of Education at two levels, Ordinary and Advanced. One unpopular change was that nobody under the age of sixteen was permitted to take the Ordinary Level, or under eighteen the Advanced Level exams. Many educationists opposed these limits and expressed their views in the local papers and the age restrictions were later removed.

In the first years of peace there was a great demand for further education

176 (above)   The Great Hall,
Latymer School

177 (right)   New building at
Latymer School opened by HM
Queen Mother in 1966

courses, both evening and part-time. Men and women, many of whose education had been interrupted by the war, were keen to acquire new skills and qualifications. There were technical courses in subjects such as electrical and mechanical engineering, technical drawing and metalwork and a wide range of commercial ones including accountancy, bookkeeping, typing, shorthand and modern languages, in each of the three boroughs. For those who wanted to improve their domestic skills there was cookery, handicrafts, dressmaking and decorating.

The 1950s was a time of sixth-form expansion as more university places became available and new universities were established. However, many pupils, including a significant number from the Latymer School, continued to drop out of education at fifteen, the school leaving age, as they could easily obtain employment. In 1953 Minchenden School reported that seventy of their former pupils were at universities but the Latymer School in 1957 was concerned that only seven of its pupils intended to go on to higher education. Funds from the Latymer Foundation were then made available to poorer students to encourage them to continue their studies and in 1965 the number of school leavers obtaining university places had risen to thirty-seven with forty-eight others entering other higher education institutions such as colleges of technology or colleges of education. Most of these girls chose to train as teachers. There was a big expansion of tertiary education places in the 1960s when thirty polytechnics were created, including Middlesex Polytechnic based at Trent Park but with campuses all over North London. Enfield Technical College was also re-organised and upgraded to offer degree courses in technical subjects such as engineering. Southgate College moved to a new building and expanded its range of courses of further education. The eminent local horticulturist, Frances Perry, an EPS Vice-President, suggested to LBE that it should use the badly neglected Capel Manor to train craftsmen gardeners who were mostly employed in public parks. The grounds and some of the outbuildings were leased to the council and the first students arrived in 1968 to study for City and Guilds qualifications one day a week.

The mid-1960s saw the start of a movement to ensure that teachers reinforced and developed their professional skills by further training, either locally or by secondments on national courses. This led to the creation of Teachers' Centres which provided a setting for a programme of courses and discussion groups, largely determined by the teachers themselves.

In 1965 Middlesex County Council was abolished and in London the administration of education was passed to the recently created London boroughs, including the London Borough of Enfield. Douglas Denny, formerly Edmonton's Education Officer, was appointed Chief Education Officer with Maurice Healey of Southgate as his deputy. By this time the division of children into three categories, the academically able, technical workers and the rest was discredited and there were serious doubts about the accuracy of the eleven plus tests in determining the difference between academic ability and technical aptitude. Five per cent of children went to private schools, 25 per cent to grammar schools and the rest to secondary moderns where they rarely took any exams or gained any qualifications. Circular 10/65, issued by the Ministry of Education, did not abolish the eleven plus selection procedures but invited local education authorities to

178. Enfield
Grammar School

draw up plans for the introduction of comprehensive education. The recently established London Borough of Enfield agreed to comply with the Ministry circular, so the first task was to prepare a plan for the re-organisation of secondary education throughout the borough. Many teachers, schoolchildren and parent welcomed the advent of comprehensive schools but there was opposition from other members of these groups. Forty-four members of the staff of Enfield County School sent a protest to the local press which stated: 'We of the County School wish to support publicly all who have protested against a wholesale switch to a comprehensive system'. In 1966 the Joint Parents' Emergency Committee was formed and there were protest marches to the Civic Centre. At first the plan was to close the successful Enfield Central School and amalgamate Enfield Grammar and Chace Boys, Enfield County and Chace Girls, Ambrose Fleming Technical Grammar and Ponders End Girls, St Ignatius and Cardinal Allen, Holy Family and St Angela's Convents, Suffolk and Minchenden Schools, Southgate County and Oakwood, Edmonton County and Rowantree. Some grammar schools determined to fight the proposed change of status. The Governors of the Latymer School, Edmonton, had already expressed their rejection of the comprehensive plan on the grounds that the Latymer endowment 'was the birthright of every child in the parish to the end of the world'. A compromise plan was finally agreed which allowed it to remain a grammar school with selective entry but the catchment area was extended to the whole of the borough. A big rebuilding project was then planned with new science laboratories, gyms, music and art rooms which were opened by Elizabeth, the Queen Mother, in 1966.

Meanwhile, some of the parents of children at the other grammar schools determined to fight on. The foundation governors of Enfield Grammar School had voted unanimously in August 1965 to oppose the change but the council-appointed governors, who were the majority, voted in favour. A petition with 10,000 signatures against the scheme was presented to Parliament by local MPs Iain Macleod and Anthony Berry. In December the Minister of Education, Anthony Greenwood, rejected the council's proposals because they included schools on split sites but a revised scheme was approved in February 1967. The Joint Parents Committee then resorted to the law with financial backing from parents, Old Grammarians and local businesses. When the judge refused to grant an injunction, it was decided to appeal and the Court of Appeal had no hesitation in finding for the Parents' Committee and awarding costs against Enfield Council. However there were further delays and confusion and the Minister of Education, now Patrick Gordon-Walker, intervened with the proposal to amend the articles of government of the Grammar School and allowed only four days for objections to be heard. After objections to the timing, this was extended to four weeks but in the end it was agreed that all secondary education in the borough would, in future, be comprehensive with the exception of the Latymer School. The protests, however, did not cease: in January 1968 some Enfield Grammar School parents threw 'a toilet roll, pennies and a tanner [sixpence]' from the public gallery into the Council Chamber during a meeting of the Education Committee because seventy-two boys had been transferred to Chace School.

By the end of the 1960s most eleven-year-old children were transferring from primary to comprehensive schools and despite a change of Government early in the next decade, when Mrs Thatcher was Minister of Education, the comprehensive system remained.

Chapter 9

Industry & Manufacturing

From the early years of the twentieth century onwards industry had been well established in the Enfield area as the River Lea provided power and was an ideal highway for both raw materials and finished goods. New industries were also encouraged by the expansion of the northern outer London suburbs. Pioneering companies such as Ediswan and Belling already had a long history of successful development and production in Enfield which had become a focal point for electronic and civil engineering firms in the early decades of the century. This was accelerated with the construction of the A10 Great Cambridge Road and the A406 North Circular Road in

179   Brimsdown Power Station

180 (above)   Ponders End Gasworks

181 (below)   An aerial view of industrial Enfield

182.   *Two kilns at the Cornish Brickworks, Hoe Lane*

183   *Clay moulding machinery*

184   Prisoners-of-war working at a local nursery

185   Local produce — the late Colin Thompson at Thompson's Nursery

186   Women workers on a tank made in Enfield

the 1920s, which provided much improved access to and through the area and created ideal new sites for industry. Power for industry, domestic use and street lighting was provided, principally, by the Brimsdown Power Station and by the Ponders End Gasworks. The latter was bombed and had to be completely rebuilt in 1949 when it was regarded as one of the most up-to-date in Britain.

By 1939 there were a number of factories on the A10 between Carterhatch Lane and the extensive Crown Brick Works on the corner of Southbury Road: these included Cosmocord, British Sangamo and Belling & Lee. There was also a concentration of factories in Queensway, Ponders End, including E. & E. Kaye, Stadium Ltd and the Standard Fuse Company, with similar pockets in Edmonton and across the region from Enfield Lock in the east to New Southgate in the west.

Brickmaking was a long standing traditional industry in Enfield and this continued to prosper on a number of sites throughout this period, mainly in north-east Enfield, and finally ceased only in 1976. Horticulture, which was mainly based in the Lea Valley, had long produced vegetables and fruits for the London markets. Food production had greatly increased during the war and this industry was still successful in the immediate post-war years but then started to face stiff competition with the influx of cheaper vegetables and fruit from overseas.

Following the outbreak of war in 1939 many local companies switched production to assist the war effort, usually by Government direction, and they helped to make a significant contribution to the eventual outcome. The following is a selection of those companies and the war work they undertook.

187   Ponders End Flour Mill

Wrights Flour Mill, Ponders End, was under Government control throughout the war and production was increased to help secure food supplies for the nation and to compensate for the losses caused by the bombing of the London Docks. The mill worked seven days a week for fifty-two weeks a year throughout the war.

Express Motor & Body Works Ltd, Great Cambridge Road, was ordered to switch from motor body building and vehicle maintenance to aircraft construction, making two intermediate wing sections and the complete tail plane for the Halifax bomber; staff numbers increased from 400 to 2,000, of whom 50 per cent were women. The factory had to be restructured and manufactured its own jigs and tools.

Ripaults Ltd, Southbury Road, switched production from electrical cables to automobile and aircraft cables. Millions of yards of cables were made for tanks, trucks, wheeled vehicles and searchlights, with similar yardage of screened cables for radar and aircraft. The factory area was increased by 25 per cent and part-time female labour was employed.

188   *Ripault's Factory*

Peto Scott Electrical Instruments Ltd, Great Cambridge Road, made direction finding equipment and mine detectors; their waterproof mine detector was a vital factor for the D-Day landings — transported in water tight containers ahead of the invasion forces. A new factory was opened in Sarnesfield Road and a factory in Windmill Hill was staffed almost entirely by housewives working part time.

Belling & Lee Ltd, Great Cambridge Road, produced five million fuses a year for radar. Air intervention equipment production for night fighters was transported to North Weald aerodrome where it was collected by aircraft from all over England.

Cosmos Manufacturing Co Ltd, Brimsdown, made radio valves and cathode-ray tubes for radar which helped in the Battle of Britain and in precision bombing of priority targets in Germany.

J W Spear & Sons Ltd, Brimsdown, switched from manufacturing games to parts for machine guns, tank fittings and pontoon bridge components.

Enfield Cables Ltd manufactured cables for ack ack, anti-aircraft artillery gun sites and hundreds of miles of cables for the RAF, the Navy and for D-Day.

Chaseside Engineering Co Ltd, Great Cambridge Road, produced mechanical shovels, mobile cranes, dumpers and shunting tractors, the same products as pre-war but the dumper was re-designed to fit on to the Fordson Industrial Tractor.

Edison Swan Electric Light Co Ltd manufactured accumulators to power submarines, valves for telecommunications, medical instruments and special wires for the enormous output of lamps and valves. In 1939 the workforce totalled 604 but during the war more than 200 additional staff were working under supervision in their own homes, garages and small shops and there was a total production of 8 million lamps up to 1945.

Belling & Co, Bridge Works, Southbury Road, by 1939 occupied 200,000 square feet and employed more than 500 workers. During the war the factory was taken over for the construction of wartime equipment: radar components, hand and rifle grenades, airfield landing lights, anti-vibration trays for bombers and VHF aerials for aircraft. In preparation for D-Day the company produced thousands of air warmers for the merchant ships which would be taking part.

Industry of this area was a regular target for German bombers and the Bell Equipment factory was one of many destroyed in air raids.

During the war and up to 1955 local industry was booming. Despite the fluctuations in the economy, the immediate post-war years saw a huge demand for electrical goods and other consumer durables which ensured comparative prosperity and high levels of employment in the Enfield area. One of the main problems for local firms was a shortage of labour and in the early 1950s the papers, week by week, carried many advertisements for unfilled vacancies.

189   The bombed Bell Equipment factory

In 1946 Ferguson's started to manufacture television sets and with the rapid demand for this product, a new purpose-built factory was constructed on the corner of Southbury Road and the A10. By 1947 there were more than 100 factories in Enfield manufacturing in excess of 1,000 products. Each week 1,000 tons of copper were being refined, and cookers, lamps, radio sets and cables were taking the names of Enfield's electrical manufacturers all over the world. These companies included Belling & Co Ltd which was manufacturing heating, cooking and water heating equipment; Belling & Lee Ltd: radio and electrical components; Edison Swan Electric Co Ltd: electrical equipment; Ferguson Radio Corporation Ltd: radio and electrical equipment; Johnson Matthey & Co Ltd: melters, assayers, bullion refiners and engineers specialising in precious metals; Ripaults Ltd: electric cables, automobile equipment and accessories; Ruberoid Co Ltd: bituminous building materials; Sangamo Weston Ltd: electrical engineers; Tricity Cookers Ltd: electric domestic cooking and heating apparatus.

Local companies have received only a brief mention, but the following gives a more detailed description of the activities during the period 1939 to 1969 of three major industries in the area — in the west, Standard Telephones and Cables, based in New Southgate and now just over the boundary with the London Borough of Barnet, employed a great many staff from Enfield and Southgate: the Royal Small Arms Factory at Enfield Lock in the east and the British Oxygen Company in Angel Road, Edmonton, in the south.

190 & 191
Television
sets being
manufactured
at Ferguson's
factory

Standard Telephones and Cables (STC), New Southgate. The company was originally established in 1883 as an agency of the American giant, Western Electric, to market the telephone. In 1925 Western Electric was bought by International Telephone and Telegraph Company (ITT) and the British part of the company was changed to STC. By then, in 1922, a 27-acre site had been purchased in New Southgate, and by 1939 additional land had been acquired expanding the site to 40 acres with 15 acres of floor space developed for manufacturing, mostly telephone exchanges and radios. With the threat of war looming shelter tunnels were dug for air raid protection; these contained every facility for the staff and had a total capacity of 5,000. In July 1938 STC was the only company invited to a secret conference

192   *The busy Belling Bridge Works in the 1960s*

on communications, with a proposal to ring the country with telephone circuits to ensure that nowhere was isolated and beyond the reach of central authority in the event of war. As at other local factories and work places, a Local Defence Volunteer force, (later called the Home Guard), was formed initially with 200 men but later increased to 400. At the outbreak of war many STC workers were directed to stay in their jobs, in reserved occupations. One million square feet of vital production space was camouflaged with netting to fox enemy bombers, and this blended into the 37 acres of landscaped gardens. The production of selenium rectifier discs expanded from 500,000 in 1939 to 23 million in 1944 (these converted an alternating current supply to direct current — needed for army radios, battery chargers and aircraft engine starters).

During the war period there were many vital developments and production lines at STC. The Standard Beam Approach System for aircraft landing was developed, which became standard equipment for Bomber Command. The Fleet Air Arm requested small radio-telegraph sets for fighter aircraft for reconnaissance, and 2,140 were made and supplied. Radar transmitters were supplied at a rate of twenty-nine a month. Another important development was the Stations Type 9000 Transmitter and Modulator for guiding aircraft with extreme accuracy to their target and then giving the precise moment at which bombs should be dropped; this enabled the Krupps factory at Essen to be hit for the first time. Throughout the war, from research and development engineering through to manufacturing and supply expertise, there was an excellent working relationship between the company, the armed services and various ministries.

By late 1943 the number of employees at New Southgate had increased to 10,500, supplemented by a large number of home-workers who carried out light assembly inspection work. Although the factories at New Southgate had suffered little damage in the first four years of the war, this changed dramatically on 23 August 1944, when a V1 Flying Bomb hit the site at 7.59am, causing devastating damage to two buildings in which a considerable number of employees were at their workplaces; this resulted in horrific casualties. Officially this was the worst V1 incident of the war with thirty-three dead and over 200 injured. Incredibly the very next day another V1 crashed on the site but this time on the North Field, resulting in little damage apart from blown-out windows.

At the end of the war STC was well placed to tackle the challenge of translating wartime technological advances into peacetime commercial applications. The number of employees had peaked in 1943 at 10,500 and although reduced to 9,000 by the end of the war this still represented a huge community with tremendous expertise and potential. The Tele-communications Authority in the UK was the Post Office, with which the

193   Aerial view of the Standard Telephone and Cables site, New Southgate in 1940

194   30-tonne presses at STC in 1940

195   Wartime camouflage netting on STC Building No 3

196   STC Building No 6 was destroyed by a V1 rocket on 23 August 1944

Telephone Division at STC had a long-standing and comfortable relationship and whose task was to continue the extension of the telephone network throughout the country. In 1950 this division installed the largest private telephone exchange to date in a new Government office with 3,000 internal lines and thirty-three manual positions. The company also developed an automatic system for the booking of aircraft passenger seats (ABEX), and designed and made a wide range of equipment for the increasing range of British-built civil and military aircraft.

There was a need for more intensive training and re-training of staff. Courses were set up for graduates joining straight from college, and an increasing number of apprenticeships were offered. There was a very well supported Athletics and Social Club: the main games were cricket, rugby, football, bowls, tennis, swimming and hockey. The 1948 Olympic Games in London included three employees of STC Southgate.

In 1949 the STC New Southgate Radio Engineering Society (RES) was

197   *The shop floor at STC*

formed. The Radio Division's new products included ground navigational aids, radio link control terminals and aerial ancillaries and relays. The company was a pioneer of precision approach radar and developed subscriber trunk dialling (STD) and international subscriber dialling (ISD). By 1962 STC had supplied airborne equipment, VHF communications and navigation systems worth well over £1 million to Eastern European companies.

In 1963 New Southgate was working on sixty-nine telephone exchanges and continuing development on electronic exchanges. The Standard Telephones Advanced Radio Telephone (Starphone) was being developed as a range of private mobile radios, including a pocket portable, with Tony Langston as one of the Team Leaders. Meanwhile, development started on the TXE4 telephone exchange with electronic switching — the first big step in the national telephone revolution and the shape of things to come.

The Royal Small Arms Factory (RSAF), Enfield Lock, was a Government owned arms manufacturer built by order of the Board of Ordnance towards the end of the Napoleonic War on an island site between the River Lea and the River Lea Navigation. In 1935 the Lewis gun was replaced by a light automatic Czechoslovak-designed machine gun; this Brno-Enfield collaboration produced the .303 Bren gun. In the two years up to January 1939 the number employed at the RSAF increased from 900 to 3,400 and by that date the Bren gun was in full production on a wartime scale. King George VI visited the factory in 1940 and tried out the weapon.

It was realised that at this time there was an increased need for an enhanced supply of high quality skilled craftsmen and to help bridge this gap a more formal training scheme for the apprentices would be necessary with a structured programme of training under a series of masters with a range of skills. In 1942 an Apprentice Training Centre was opened in which first-year apprentices were given high quality foundation courses of basic engineering before moving into the workshops as trade apprentices who would become either skilled craftsmen or professional engineers and future managers.

With the outbreak of World War II there had been an increase in the production of components for the Bren gun, the Vickers machine gun, the .38 revolver, and for a variety of other weapons while the repair of rifles continued. The factory had set up its own ARP and Home Guard and, in the anticipation of air raids, steel panelled shelters, covered with earth, were constructed. The industrial area from Ponders End to the Royal Gunpowder Factory at Waltham Abbey was an obvious target for German bombers and a parachute mine caused substantial damage to a number of RSAF buildings on 21 November 1940.

With the loss of so many weapons which had to be abandoned on the retreat

198 The Royal Small Arms Factory Machine Shop and attached range

199   Bren gun production line

of our troops to Dunkirk, it became necessary to establish additional weapons production in other factories, and the tool room and small-arms inspectorate at RSAF had a significant role in setting this up. The Pattern Room was moved to Broxbourne, the wartime headquarters of the Chief Inspector of Small-Arms, where it co-ordinated the work of many small engineering companies and kept them up to date with design changes and improvements by issuing

200   Assembling a Bren gun at the RSAF

201   King George VI firing a Bren gun on a visit to RSAF in 1940

202   *Straightening gun barrels was a specific skill*

sample drawings and components. The number of workers continued to expand to reach 6,315, with many women employed, often at skilled work such as examiners and viewers; shift working was adopted from the beginning of the war. At its peak, output reached 10,000 Bren guns, 1,000 revolvers and 1,000 Sten guns a week. (Sten stood for Shepherd-Turpin-England, while in other weapons, such as the Bren, the 'en' stood for Enfield.)

The Sten gun was designed by Harold Turpin, the Senior Design Draughtsman at RSAF, in December 1940, following the Dunkirk evacuation, when it was realised that the British Forces did not have any submachine guns in service. He evolved a simple design which could be made quickly and cheaply with minimal machining needs which he described to Major Shepherd, Head of the RSAF Design Section during WW2. Lord Beaverbrook, the minister responsible for armament production ordered that prototypes should be made and by 8 January 1941 the first Sten gun was completed. The Prime Minister, Winston Churchill, tried out the new gun on a visit in June 1941. Orders were given to get it into large scale production and by the end of 1941 over 500,000 men had been armed with the Sten gun.

Once the war in Europe ended in 1945 no new armament orders were placed by the Government with the ordnance factories, which by then numbered forty-four. They had to rely on alternative work to survive which at Enfield Lock, included carpenters' tools and plumbing equipment to assist in the post-war house rebuilding. The number of employees dropped

203   Apprentice training at the RSAF

dramatically. In 1948 weapon designers at RSAF started to develop the first bullpup rifle, the EM2; it was recognised as a potential world class innovation but its development was stopped in 1952 by Winston Churchill who wanted army small arms to be supplied by Belgium to assist that country's post-war recovery.

In June 1950 the Korean War began when North Korea invaded the South and this forced the British Government to increase defence expenditure and to get the ordnance factories back to full scale production. Enfield benefited, despite the difficulty in recruiting sufficient new workers, with the transfer of all Hispano cannon production from Poole in 1952 and the introduction of new modern machine tools. Although this war ended in 1953, the number of employees at Enfield Lock increased as the Cold War intensified, and at 31 March 1956 the number had reached 1,497, and the year's production had exceeded £1 million. A national apprenticeship scheme was created to serve all the Royal Ordnance Factories and other defence establishments, modelled on the success of the RSAF one which was further expanded in 1967 when a

204   The RSAF site was damaged twice by enemy action

new training centre was opened to accommodate the thirty 'new starters' each year.

With the successful development of the British hydrogen bomb in 1957, the Government warned that production of weapons at the ordnance factories would contract and that some factories would be closed. However this had little effect on the RSAF at Enfield Lock which then took over work from some of the closed factories such as Poole and Fazakerley. Production work at Enfield was now almost exclusively carried out by men, with women restricted to certain ancillary tasks. Recruitment was still mostly through the apprenticeship system. The factory held an annual exhibition of apprentice work and prize giving, which was attended by representatives from the colleges where the apprentices undertook day release courses.

National Service ended in 1962 and the contraction of production predicted in 1957 began to affect RSAF. Much of the northern part of the site at Enfield Lock was closed down and production was concentrated in the buildings at the southern end. The No 4 Short Magazine Lee Enfield rifle was now superseded by the self-loading rifle, and in August 1966 a coffin containing the rifle was buried with full military honours on the rifle range at Bisley. The function of the ordnance factories, including Enfield, was now to provide the main reserve capacity to meet possible emergencies. Further reorganisation was carried out between 1967 and 1969 when all the workshops east of the canal were transferred to the main part of the factory west of the canal. But by 1969 the writing was already on the wall and the site was completely closed in 1988

205   Ministry of Defence Pattern Room at the RSAF

206   The Prime Minister, Winston Churchill, tries out the Sten gun. The designer, Harold Turpin is on the far left.

207   RSAF Machine Shop 7 in 1947

208   Precision casting by the lost wax technique

209 Machine Shop 2 producing the self-loading rifle in late 1950s

British Oxygen Company (BOC), Edmonton, celebrated its golden anniversary in 1936, with the Angel Road Edmonton plant having been widely recognised, over many years, for its engineering excellence and innovation. In the 1930s BOC was producing gas in twenty UK factories, but at Edmonton, in addition to gases, they were producing gas manufacturing plant, welding and cutting gear and medical equipment. General fabrication services were also provided,

210   Oxygen tankers at BOC

including sheet metal and press work, machining, die casting and wire weaving. The site then extended over 20 acres with more than half covered by buildings and workshops.

With the outbreak of war in 1939 the specialist skills at Angel Road were adapted to provide welding, cutting and medical equipment for the armed forces; mini oxygen producing plants were manufactured for the RAF, which were used to provide supplies for high altitude flying, when it was not possible to deliver cylinders in war zones such as North Africa.

In the immediate post-war years changes in steel making technology, and other industrial developments, resulted in an increased demand for oxygen. BOC set up a Process Development Department to study ways of meeting the higher demand, while improving plant efficiency and lowering operating costs. Coil-wound heat exchangers were constructed in copper, but when columns became larger in the 1950s, sections were cast in phosphor bronze or a proprietary brand of zinc and brass alloy. As components grew in size, and became available from specialist manufacturers, the Edmonton plant ceased to make these ancillary parts and concentrated on fabricating air separation columns, cold boxes and pipework. With the increased need to store and transport liquid gases, large spheres were developed, cast from bronze in two halves, which were then encased in a carbon steel outer sphere, with insulation in the space between the two. In the early 1950s there was a name change to the Chemical Plant Division of British Oxygen Engineering Ltd. In parallel with the construction of new workshops, the bridges over Salmons Brook were replaced, where it flowed through the site.

In 1956 on-site facilities for apprentices were introduced; about 125 apprentices studied at the training centre and subsequently they would fabricate plant, follow it to the customer's site, complete the construction, then participate in the start-up and commissioning of the plant. In 1961 the

211 A Glenman's cold box manufactured at BOC, Edmonton

range of BOC tankers built at Edmonton was rationalised to three types — a 2,900m³ sphere, a 8,400m³ tank insulated with powder, and a 4,200m³ vacuum insulated tank. Four years later the Research and Development Department designed one of the first helium refrigerators for the Rutherford High Energy Laboratory at Didcot. This was capable of maintaining a temperature of -270°C for up to thirty days. With the increasing demand for ever larger vacuum insulated evaporators and vacuum insulated tanks, the Edmonton Angel Road site soon needed further expansion and investment to meet the growing needs of national and international customers.

In 1947 the success and strength of local industry was evident when the Enfield & District Manufacturers' Association organised the 'Enfield Can Do It' exhibition; this featured seventy companies which exported their products from Enfield to all parts of the world.

Industry and manufacturing in the area continued to flourish over the next few years and in May 1954 Ripaults claimed that in every British car there was an Enfield product, but there were worrying signs for the future. At an industrial conference in 1955, a director of Ediswans said that two outstanding problems for industry were the shortage of manpower, especially engineers, and the lack of new techniques.

During the 1950s the Clean Air Act and the convenience of electricity increased greatly the demand for electric cookers and fires. One of the main

212   Programme of the 'Enfield Can Do It' exhibition

beneficiaries was Belling at their Southbury Road Bridge Works but demand for these products increased to such an extent that the company had to build a factory at Burnley to cope with soaring sales.

In 1956 the slow but inevitable decline of industry in the area began; Ferguson laid off 600 workers as demand for televisions declined. By the end of the decade Britain's industrial output was growing more slowly than that of many other countries and our share of world markets was declining. Inevitably this affected many companies in the area, such as AEC Lighting which had to lay off 300 employees in 1962 as a result of a cut back in production. In 1963 AEI closed the historic Ediswan works at Ponders End as it had become increasingly unsuitable for modern electrical manufacturing

There were some bright spots in the final years of this period. Among these the knighthood awarded to Jules Thorn and the new apprentice training centre, opened by his company at its Great Cambridge Road works, to provide 50 first year training places for craft and technical apprentices. In the same year this company developed and put into production a fully transistorised computer type colour television chassis — a world first. In 1968 three local firms won the Queen's Award for Industry for success in the export market: Universal Matthey Products, Atlas Lighting and Johnson Matthey, but the decline in British manufacturing had begun and would gather pace in the years to come.

CHAPTER 10
Enfield Preservation Society

T
he Enfield Preservation Society (EPS) was only three years old in
September 1939 but in that time it had achieved much by masterminding
the defeat of Enfield Urban District Council's plan to build a town hall,
first on Chase Green and then on Library Green. (For information about
these campaigns see Valerie Carter's *Fighting for the Future*). In 1939 EPS
membership was 130 and the annual subscription 10s 6d (52p). In the months
just before war was declared, EPS protested about the ugliness of the open
trenches dug on Library Green but this objection was withdrawn as fears grew
about air raids and possible poison gas attacks. An assurance was received
from the Council that efforts would be made to improve the appearance of
the sites once the trenches were roofed and converted into air raid shelters.
EPS also objected to the proposal to establish military camps on The Ridgeway

213   Trenches on Library Green

214   Old Vestry House railings

and Vicarage Farms because of the proximity to Chase Farm Hospital and 'better class houses'.

During the war, inevitably, other concerns took precedence but it is recorded in the *Enfield Gazette* of June 1940 that an unsightly advertisement on Windmill Hill Railway Bridge had just been removed in response to a request made by EPS in 1937! There were few meetings in the first year of the war because, as the Chairman reported at the 1940 AGM, there was little scope for action and the subscription was therefore reduced to 5s (25p). £40 of the Society's funds was invested in Defence Bonds. One success, however, was achieved by Mrs Hodson, the only woman on the Council of Management, when she reported that the decorative iron railings in front of the Old Vestry House in The Town were to be removed and melted down for munitions. They are still in place today thanks to the strong letter of protest sent by EPS.

The inertia, as one chairman later put it, when 'EPS had slumbered but not died', seems to have lasted until 1959 when the Society was propelled back into activity. Mrs Carinthia Arbuthnot Lane, who with her husband Tony had moved to Gentleman's Row, noticed white crosses on several of the mature trees in the front gardens of her road. On learning that it was proposed to cut

215 (right)   The Rev Ebenezer Rees, EPS Chairman

216 (below)   Mr & Mrs Arbuthnot Lane with Godfrey Groves

them down she wrote a strong letter to the press, saved the trees and stirred the Enfield Preservation Society to life. The Rev Ebenezer Rees, a founder member, became Chairman again with Mrs Lane as Honorary Secretary. At the first meeting the Chairman expressed the hope that 'the Society's former activities could now be resumed in cooperation with the Borough Council and the Civic Trust so that improvements to the development of the town could be achieved and amenities increased'. In March 1950 an open meeting was arranged in the Tudor Room of Little Park, Gentleman's Row, to revive

217   Don Gresswell and Christopher Jephcott clearing an overgrown footpath

218   Donald Potter and Tony Lane were among the volunteers clearing 5 tons of rubbish from Coopers Lane Road in 1963

interest and recruit new members. An advertisement about it appeared in the *Enfield Gazette* and there was a great response; the room was packed and ninety-eight new members enrolled. At the AGM which followed in June an election of members of the Council of Management was held for the first time; the pre-war members had all been nominated. Younger people from a range of professions and backgrounds were elected to replace 'the local worthies', including two who were to play major roles in the revival of the Society, Don Gresswell and Donald Potter. The subscription was fixed at 2s 6d (12.5p) and membership rose to 200. The Chairman of FERRA (Federation of Enfield Residents and Ratepayers' Associations) complained that there were no representatives of Eastern Enfield elected. He advised members of FERRA not to join EPS 'because it was trying to revive a corpse' but to wait and join instead the proposed new amenity society which had been suggested by a former Mayor of Enfield. This was launched a year later in March 1961 as The Enfield Society but lasted for only two years. In October 1963 the *Enfield Weekly Herald* reported that the Enfield Society had written to EPS suggesting amalgamation. By this time EPS had 750 members whereas the Enfield Society had only eighty-two. The two societies were formally amalgamated in 1964.

Donald Potter was elected chairman in 1961 and the Rev Rees became the first president. The aims and objectives of EPS were revised to include the protection of the green belt which had been established round London in the late 1920s. These remain virtually unchanged today:

- to preserve and improve the amenities of Enfield
- to defend the Green Belt from encroachment
- to protect any local place or building of beauty or historic interest
- to preserve footpaths in and around Enfield
- to encourage good design in the development of the Borough.

Until 1965 activities were concentrated on Enfield as Edmonton and Southgate were separate boroughs.

The years 1962-7 were dominated by opposition to the Town Development Plan proposed by Enfield Council. The suggested route of the three lane ring road, the purpose of which was to reduce traffic congestion in The Town, was through the ancient graveyard of St Andrew's church and close to the Vicarage, through the Grammar School grounds, Holly Walk, part of the New River, Cecil Road and Church Lane. EPS called a meeting and twenty organisations sent delegates who set up a fighting committee, known as the Save Enfield Campaign, with Mrs Lane as secretary. Seven thousand residents signed the first letter of protest. EPS wrote to Enfield Council to express its opposition to the scheme as did others including the Grammar School Old Boys Association, local clergy — the Vicar of St Andrews called the proposal 'ungodly' — and many individuals. In March 1963 the council set up an exhibition about the scheme at the newly opened Civic Centre but the *Enfield Gazette*'s report on this warned readers of the consequences of the implementation of the plan saying 'Down will come 400 houses, a score of shops and offices and at least three public houses — a wholesale extirpation that even the Luftwaffe [the German Air Force] could not achieve'. Enfield Council, however, approved the plan and went ahead and demolished the Victorian cottages in Church Lane and replaced them with a car park. Middlesex County Council gave its

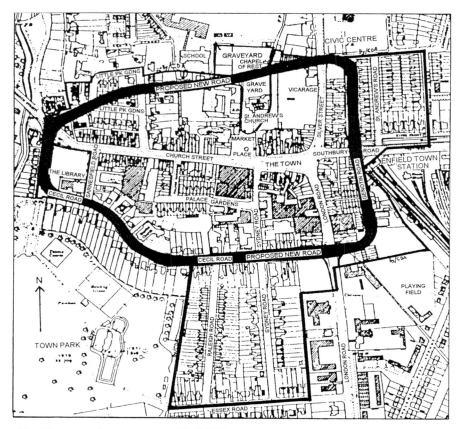

219   *The proposed ring road round Enfield Town*

approval just before its abolition. The comment in the *Enfield Gazette* on this action was; 'If the MCC is so out of touch with local opinion to approve a redevelopment plan that has appalled residents, ratepayers, shopkeepers, industrialists, women's organisations and the Preservation Society, it is perhaps not a bad thing that it is going to disappear under the local government re-organisation'.

Meanwhile the protest campaign was gathering momentum and £279 was raised as a fighting fund. EPS helped by organising regular displays in the Market Place and by putting stakes in the ground showing the proposed northern route through the graveyard. By May, 9,700 people had signed the protest and David Napley was retained as the Save Enfield Action Committee's legal representative. He warned that the cost to the committee of the public enquiry would be at least £2,000. There was only £641 in the kitty so fund-raising activities were set up, including a market stall. EPS then asked William Palmer, chairman of its Architecture and Planning Group, to produce an alternative plan to ease the chronic traffic congestion in The Town area without destroying its historic heart. He drew up a scheme of a bypass just to the south of Cecil Road through to Old Park Avenue but his

220 The listed Vicarage was on the route of the proposed ring road

221 Demolition of cottages in Church Lane

222   White stakes showing the proposed route of the ring road

idea was not popular as it would have affected the Town Park. Alan Skilton
of EPS built a detailed architectural model of Enfield of the suggested route
which is now in the Museum of London. Even a few members of the EPS
Council of Management were not in favour of this scheme and it has been
suggested that this was because of what we would now call 'nimbyism'. The
Save Enfield Action Committee, also, did not endorse the EPS proposal, so
what is described as 'a curt letter' was sent to them reminding them that
EPS had contributed a considerable sum towards the cost of the legal and
professional services to fight the plan and that they had a viable alternative
plan prepared which would not destroy the historic centre of Enfield.
EPS also warned that they might withdraw support from the Save Enfield
Campaign and 'go it alone'. Objections had to be submitted to the Council
by 25 January 1965 and EPS protested on behalf of its 1,059 members.
The Borough Planning Committee was shown the model of the alternative
scheme and accepted 'a need to minimise the visual and aural effects of
the northern ring road'. Their suggested proposal in May 1966 was that the
road should be sunk five feet below ground level near St Andrew's Church
and Holly Walk. This was not acceptable. Before the public enquiry could
be arranged, the opposition was boosted by an article in *The Observer* by
Ian Nairn, architecture consultant, who had earlier mentioned the plan
in his *Daily Telegraph* column. He wrote 'a true town with the market
square, leafy churchyard — any road here is out of the question'. The
Enfield Gazette headline in May 1967 was 'Saved by the Minister of Housing

223   Temple Bar

and Local Government: Borough town plan thrown out' while the *Enfield Herald* reported that the Minister, Anthony Greenwood, had rejected the plan without a public enquiry. The gyratory one-way system which we have today was to be implemented rather than the one suggested by EPS. It was a victory for the Save Enfield Campaign and all who had contributed were thanked, but Mrs Lane of EPS was singled out for 'her enthusiasm, drive and unceasing work'. The fighting fund had risen to £1,000 and the unspent balance was placed in a special account, administered by EPS, and has since been used to fight other threats. The one-way gyratory system finally came into force in Enfield Town in 1969. However, in the EPS's December *Newsletter* Christopher Jephcott wrote that EPS was disappointed that the scheme, although successful, had been achieved only at the cost of much damage to the atmosphere and appearance of The Town and some EPS suggestions about street clutter and signs were later implemented.

Although this campaign must have taken up a great deal of EPS's committee members' time and energy for six years, EPS was simultaneously developing new activities. In 1960 it was represented for the first time at a local planning enquiry, opposed the replacement of the Victorian fountain in Enfield Town by a flower bed and mounted a campaign to have the neglected and deteriorating Temple Bar restored and relocated in the City of London. (This was not achieved until 2004). Four groups were formed in September

224 (above)   First EPS Newsletter

225 (right)   An early EPS
Christmas card

226 (far right)   Footpath Map

1963: Footpaths and Open Spaces Group initiated by Don Gresswell, a Trees
Group led by Christopher Jephcott (the current President of the Enfield
Society), Architecture and Planning Group led briefly by Robert Gowers
and then by William Palmer: and the Historic Buildings Group headed by
Mrs Lane. She also issued the first *Newsletter*, a duplicated typewritten sheet.
In the same year there was a campaign which has a familiar ring about it,
to get rid of street clutter such as too many signposts, railings and other
obstructions.

Publishing was a new enterprise for the Society. The first Christmas card
was produced for sale in 1963 and there has been a new one almost every
year since. The first Footpath Map, published in 1964, proved so popular that
it was reprinted in 1966 and has been revised and reprinted regularly since
as new footpaths have been opened. Cuthbert Whitaker's 1911 *A History of
Enfield* was reproduced in 1965 and sold so well that it was reprinted. In 1968
the first guided walk leaflet 'A Guide to Enfield Town', appeared and it also
has been revised several times. Its publication coincided with the first guided
walking tour of Enfield Town on which there were 300 participants and two
members dressed as Charles and Mary Lamb for the occasion. Profits from the
sale of its publications helped to finance the society's expanding activities as
they have done every year since.

The 1,000th member joined EPS in 1964 and the new groups embarked
on several initiatives. Don Gresswell set up a campaign to establish a network
of footpaths in the nearby countryside and working parties removed rubbish
from various sites. At Gough Park it took nineteen winter weekends of hard
work to cut back the undergrowth, clear the rubbish and restore the footpath
to Whitewebbs Lane. North Enfield Ratepayers joined EPS volunteers to
clear 15 tons of rubbish from one of the oldest footpaths in Enfield, from
Canonbury Cottages to Myddelton Avenue. Amongst the items removed were
bedsteads, bicycles, oil drums and prams. In 1964, at the request of Ponders

227 (right) 'Charles and Mary Lamb' on a guided walk

228 (below) The restored Gough Park footpath

*229 & 230   Two of the sites earmarked for the Ponders End clean-up by local residents and
EPS volunteers*

End Residents, EPS helped them clear seventeen tons of rubbish from that
part of the borough. Many old footpaths had been ploughed up for food
production during the Dig for Victory campaign of the war years. A map
of some of the lost paths provoked interest at the annual Town Show and
the local papers reported that 'There are more than 100 public paths within
the Borough boundaries: It is one of the aims of the Enfield Preservation

231   The display for the 1963 Enfield Town Show

Society to get these opened up to the public again'. As a result, many people supplied information on paths they remembered from the pre-war years. The first new footpath sign and stile were erected on the path from Coopers Lane Road via Holly Hill Farm to The Ridgeway and by 1964 all Enfield's country paths had been signposted by the Footpaths Group. The Society's detailed plan for an Enfield footpath network was submitted to the Borough Council with 15 miles of new paths. According to the *Enfield Weekly Herald* of April 1965, this scheme was the first to be put forward for London's Green Belt. The Footpaths Group was also involved in another pilot project when it waymarked paths on the 500-acre farm at Nazeing, owned by John Mackie, an Enfield MP. The *Enfield Gazette* reported on this and explained 'Waymarking is a system widely used on the Continent to enable visitors to see the best of the scenery by footpath without fear of losing their way. The Preservation Society is anxious to see if it helps townspeople to obtain greater enjoyment in the countryside'. Horse riding became popular in the 1960s and riders were avoiding busy roads by using the footpaths, causing damage and mud. The society therefore proposed a route of 10 miles of bridleway which was created but the request for a byelaw prohibiting horses being ridden on footpaths was not agreed.

232 & 233   *Clearing the old course of the New River (above) and some of the rubbish collected (below)*

The opening up of the countryside via the footpath network disclosed another problem. Piles of rubbish had been dumped, disfiguring the landscape and fly tipping was much in evidence. Large piles of dumped items were cleared from the old course of the New River in 1965. Even the council was guilty, using the ornamental lakes at Forty Hall as a rubbish tip between 1961 and 1966 until the water almost dried up. After repeated complaints from EPS and others this practice eventually stopped. On a clean-up operation, organised by Don Gresswell in 1963, five tons of rubbish were removed from Coopers Lane Road but when the volunteers returned to the site nine days later, they found twenty-four new dumps had appeared. It was obvious that public refuse sites were urgently needed, together with enforced penalties for dumping, and EPS requested these measures but no action was taken. At that time there was no charge by Enfield Council for the collection of large domestic items. However, to make the situation worse, in 1965, when the new London Borough of Enfield was created, it was decided to follow the policy of the former Edmonton and Southgate Councils and charge for the removal of large articles. EPS again asked for a refuse depot to be opened and for the charge to be dropped. Success was limited as the charge was cancelled for one year only. Some months later refuse depots were opened to the public. EPS pressed successfully for longer opening hours and the *Enfield Weekly Herald* reported: 'Since the Council decided last November to open their refuse depots on Saturday morning, over 200 deliveries have been recorded, including thirty-five cars and seventy lots of furniture'.

The Footpaths and Open Spaces Group was also very concerned about

234   *Tree Planting Week at Ambrose Fleming School*

235   *EPS working party at Southbury Station*

236   *One of many oak trees cut down on The Ridgeway*

the green belt, much of which in 1960 was inaccessible to the public. Don Gresswell wrote to the local papers saying that 'the people of Enfield should make it known as widely as possible that they will resist all attempts to destroy the green belt countryside by piecemeal development'. Requests to build schools, golf courses, a motel, a housing estate and shops were opposed by the society.

In July 1961 a member reported that large oak trees were being bulldozed on the building site between Gordon Hill and Lavender Hill and it was therefore decided to feature trees in the EPS display at the Enfield Town Show and to ask members to report any threat to trees. A Trees Group was formed and attempted to improve the standard of tree pruning in local parks and streets. A programme of planting began which was to transform the bleak appearance of neglected areas, especially in Eastern Enfield. The aim was to plant 1,000 trees and *Gazette* readers were invited to contribute to the cost. EPS financed the planting of ninety-five trees in March 1964 to celebrate the ninety-fifth

237   *Little Pipers, Clay Hill*

238   St Faith's Cottage, Brigadier Hill

239 (above)   Listed building plaque

240 (right)   The first plaque being
erected in 1966 at White Lodge, Silver
Street

birthday of its president, the Rev Ebenezer Rees. Enfield Tree Planting Week was held in the following November and the appeal to industry and the public was so successful that 1,103 trees were planted. One of the earliest schemes was at Southbury Station in 1965, when trees and shrubs were planted on a 45-yard strip of rough grass alongside the down platform. Three years later trees and shrubs were planted at Enfield Town Station. The group proposed the development of a tree-lined village green on the neglected land, which was marred by abandoned allotments and piles of dumped rubbish, in front of St Michael's Hospital. In 1969 John Hannah, leader of the Trees Group, received an anonymous phone call telling him that, during the previous year, eighty mature oaks had been cut down on two farms on Enfield Chase and that more trees were to be felled on all the farms along The Ridgeway. Approval had been given by the Greater London Council, the landlords, and the Ministry of Agriculture. Immediate protests were sent with demands for replacement planting but destruction continued into the 1970s. Throughout the 1960s members of the Trees Group organised working parties twice a year to plant thousands of trees, shrubs and hedgerows. A tree nursery was set up in the garden of Gough Park Cottage, Clay Hill, the home of Robert Dugdale Sykes, a Vice-President of EPS.

When Enfield Borough's schedule of twenty-six listed building was published, the Historic Buildings Group considered it to be incomplete and submitted a list of forty others which they thought were worthy of listing because of their architectural or historic interest. The council accepted only two of these to add to their list, Little Pipers, Clay Hill and St Faith's

241   The Old Bakery, Forty Hill

242 & 243 The Crown & Horseshoes before and after the improvement scheme

Cottage, Brigadier Hill. In the *Enfield Weekly Herald* of 12 June 1964, Rupert Jarvis, Secretary of the London and Middlesex Archaeological Society, called this rejection 'outrageous'. The group also suggested the production of a small plaque to identify listed buildings. These were cast in bronze alloy by a foundry in Genotin Road and the first one was fixed in August 1966 to the wall of White Lodge, Silver Street, where it can still be seen.

On New Year's Day 1965 there was a letter from the EPS Chairman, Don Gresswell, in the local papers suggesting that the name of the Society should be changed 'as it gives the impression that the Society's thoughts are always in the past'. Like the Temple Bar relocation, this did not happen until the twenty-first century. In 1966 EPS was involved in two and a half years of negotiations with five local authorities, several residents' associations, the Ramblers' Association and others to open up a 400-yard path from Cattlegate Road to the then LBE boundary. This was eventually agreed and the path was subsequently created. Other events in this period included a joint meeting on trees with Southgate Civic Society which was well supported.

The Rev Ebenezer Rees died two days before his ninety-seventh birthday. He had been the Minister at Christ Church, Enfield, a foundation governor of Enfield Grammar School and a founder of the Enfield Preservation Society. Over 500 people attended his funeral and, as a memorial, a seat was purchased by EPS and placed in front of Christ Church, Chase Side.

The Civic Amenities Act, passed by Parliament in 1967, strengthened the laws on the protection of historic buildings and the preservation of trees. However, it came into force just too late to save the Old Bakery, Forty Hill, part of which was used as a greengrocer's shop. EPS, with the support of Enfield Council, tried to stop its demolition because they considered the

244   *Enfield Town Conservation Area*

245   Forty Hall

246   Southgate Green

247   *Devon House Winchmore Hill Green*

set of buildings to be worthy of conservation but the weatherboarded house and its outbuildings were replaced by a terrace of houses. The Act required planning authorities to identify local areas where there were groups of buildings 'of special architectural or historic interest, the character or appearance of which it is desirable to preserve or enhance'. Conservation areas had arrived and Forty Hill was to be among the first such designated areas in the borough. Enfield Council had already in 1966 suggested improvements to enhance Gentleman's Row and EPS had supported the plan. The following March the *Enfield Weekly Herald* reported that a study group had been set up at the suggestion of EPS to look into the treatment of Gentleman's Row and the surrounding area. Godfrey Groves, a member of the EPS Council of Management, was elected chairman of the Gentleman's Row Study Group which sent letters to all residents of the area and held its first meeting in April 1967. Improvements swiftly followed such as the removal of boarded fencing from the footbridge and the repainting of the Crown and Horseshoes so that by June the *Enfield Gazette* reported: 'It was a scruffy spot in a charming backwater of old Enfield. Now it has been transformed'. The scheme won a commendation for EPS in the Civic Trust Awards for 1967 and it was named as Enfield's first conservation area in October 1968. In the same month Forty Hill was similarly designated and

EPS organised a meeting in the parish hall at Maidens Bridge. More than 150 people attended to hear the Borough Planning Officer talk about practical conservation, and volunteers came forward to form the Forty Hill and Bulls Cross Study Group. EPS urged the council to set up more conservation areas and Southgate and Winchmore Hill Greens were designated, but the Clay Hill suggestion was rejected. The Conservation Advisory Group (CAG) was set up by Enfield Council in 1969 on the initiative of the Borough Planning Officer with members representing EPS, FERRA. Southgate Civic Society, the study groups, Edmonton Hundred Historical Society, councillors and council officers. They were to make recommendations and suggestions about new conservation areas, improvements to existing ones and to consider any applications for developments or changes within them. They recommended three further areas, Church Street Edmonton, Ponders End Flour Mills and Vicars Moor Lane, Winchmore Hill and these were all designated as conservation areas the following year.

By the end of the 1960s the Enfield Preservation Society was a thriving organisation with 1,700 members and many activities, most of which continue to this day. As in its first years much had been achieved in a comparatively short time and a solid base established for the future, thanks to a group of dedicated volunteers.

CHAPTER 11

Epilogue — The Changed Scene

Any resident who had left the Enfield area at the outbreak of war in September 1939 and did not return until 1969 would find many changes. The street scene would look unfamiliar. Bombs had destroyed many buildings and other houses had been demolished by the local councils under slum clearance schemes. In their place were estates of modern housing, including the first tower blocks. Many small houses which were still standing and occupied had been modernised and nearly all now had bathrooms which was not the case before the war. Most homes had a television set, telephone, washing machine, refrigerator, vacuum cleaner and other electrical appliances. Large houses had been demolished in places such as The Ridgeway, Enfield, and Wellington Road, Bush Hill Park and replaced by blocks of flats. Others had been turned into old people's homes, hotels and in Chase Road, South-gate, a synagogue. Forty Hall was no longer a private residence and was open to the public: Trent Park mansion was a teacher training college. The first supermarkets would be found in shopping areas, replacing department stores and small shops. There were fewer churches: some had been converted to other uses such as housing in Winchmore Hill and Edmonton and others pulled down. The closure of public houses had also begun: The Crown Tavern and The Bell, Southgate, were among the earliest victims. About a third of cinemas were either converted to other uses, as bingo halls or supermarkets and another third had been demolished. Dance halls had also closed — Firs Hall, Winchmore Hill, was changed into a restaurant.

Another difference noticed would be the crowded roads. Few families had cars in 1939 but thirty years later the roads were so busy that car parks, yellow lines, zebra crossings and parking meters had appeared in the streets. Train engines emitting steam and cinders had been replaced by diesel or electric ones on the railways while the Underground trains were no longer red but silver. Trolleybuses had been superseded by motorised buses and the overhead lines removed.

The population had also changed as, by 1969, immigrants from Cyprus, the Indian sub-continent and the Caribbean had settled in the area. Mosques and temples were being built and Greek Orthodox churches established. Restaurants offered a wider variety of food with Indian and Chinese ones in every high street.

There were big social changes too. The depression in the 1930s had resulted in high unemployment and much poverty. The war and the immediate post-war years had provided full employment opportunities and there was a more even distribution of wealth. The Welfare State had also arrived. The general population was better housed and fed than ever before. The introduction of the National Health Service had also ensured that everyone had access to free medical, dental and optical care. Major changes in the field of education had resulted in increased numbers staying on at school past the school leaving age, which had risen to fifteen, and an increasing number going to universities. Many working families for the first time included a university graduate. This resulted in a widening of opportunities for able working class children who joined the professional classes as, for example, barristers, teachers and civil servants. Opportunities in politics were also increased: the leaders of both the major parties were grammar-school boys.

The position of women had also changed; not all ceased to work after marriage and some had jobs which had previously been the reserve of men, although they did not all receive equal pay. Top appointments included the sister of the Headmistress of Enfield County School, Dame Evelyn Sharp, the first woman to be appointed to the highest ranks of the Civil Service and Dame Elizabeth Lane the first female High Court judge. In local politics, Mrs Ruth Winston was the first lady Mayor of Southgate, Mrs Jay the first female Chairman of Enfield Urban District Council, while in 1965 Miss K. Harvey became the first Mayor of the new London Borough of Enfield.

Society in general was more liberal: the death penalty, the flogging of prisoners, the caning of children and theatre censorship had been abolished and the laws on homosexuality, abortion and divorce made less strict. People were much better dressed but there were changes — bowler hats were rarely seen, some women wore trousers and the young developed styles of their own.

There were, however, some dark clouds on the horizon. 'The Troubles' in Northern Ireland started in 1969, output from local industry was declining and had resulted in an increase in unemployment figures, crime rates were rising and strikes were becoming more frequent. The outlook for the next decade was not rosy but I shall leave it to others to write about this.

Sources & Further Reading

Birch, C. Alan, *A Brief History of Chase Farm Hospital*
Boudier, Gary, *History of the North Middlesex Hospital University Hospital*
Bowden, Geoff, *Intimate Memories*
Bray, Christopher, *1965 – The Year Modern Britain Was Born*
Carter, Valerie, *Fighting for the Future*
Christopher, John, *The London Bus Story*
Connor, J. & C., *Kings Cross to Potters Bar*
Connor, J., *Branch Lines to Enfield Town and Palace Gates*
Dalling, Graham, *The Enfield Book*
    Enfield Past
    Southgate and Edmonton Past
Dumayne, Alan, *The London Borough of Enfield*
    Fond Memories of Winchmore Hill
    Southgate — a Glimpse of the Past
    Once upon a Time in Palmers Green
Fairhurst, Doug, *A London Trolleybus Experience*
Gillam, Geoffrey, *Enfield at War 1939-45*
    Theatres, Music Halls and Cinemas in the London Borough of Enfield
Hart, Joan, *Onward Ever* (Enfield County School)
Hedgecock D., & Waite, R., *Haringey at War*
Horne, M., *The Piccadilly Line*
Lewis, Jim, *A Century of Growing*
    Gunpowder and Guns
    Weapons and Wireless
    Battleships, Buses and Bombers
Marr, Andrew, *A History of Modern Britain*
Mitchell, V. & K. Smith, *The Hertford Loop*
    Stratford to Cheshunt including the Southbury Loop
Morris, J. A., *A History of the Latymer School at Edmonton*
Neech, H. C., *Chase Farm Schools*
Pam, David, *History of Enfield Volume 3*
    The Royal Small Arms Factory and its Workers
    Enfield Town — Village Green to Shopping Precinct
    Edmonton — Ancient Village to Working Class Suburb
Schama, Simon, *A History of Britain, Volume 3*
Sellick, Stephen, *Images of England — Enfield*
Springate, Stan, *Firm Friends- Telling it like it was — the Life and Times of STC at New Southgate*

Sturges, George W., *The Silver Link 1901-57* (Silver Street Boys School, renamed Huxley County School)
    The Golden Years 1903-53 (Houndsfield School)
Taylor, R. W., *A History of a School* (Chase Side School)
White, J., *Evacuation to Essex and Beyond*
Young, E., & Jones, B. (editors), *Minchenden School Golden Anniversary 1919-69*

The Enfield Gazette, 1939-69
The Enfield Weekly Herald, 1939-69
Palmers Green & Southgate Gazette, 1939-69
Tottenham & Edmonton Weekly Herald, 1939-69
Reports of the Medical Officers of Health for Edmonton, Enfield and Southgate, 1939-65
Reports of the London Borough of Enfield Medical Officer, 1965-69
Belling and Co. Ltd — the Story of Belling 1911-62
A Brief History of Highlands Hospital
Chronicle of the Edmonton County School 1939-58
Enfield Medical Gazette, No 1
Enfield Official Programme of Victory Celebrations 1946
Fireworks, No 1. The Official Magazine of Southgate Auxiliary Fire Service
A History of BOC Process Plants in Edmonton
White Lodge Surgery

Publications of The Enfield Society Currently Available

A History of Enfield (David Pam):
    Volume ll A Victorian Suburb (1837-1914)   £17.95
Volume lll A Desirable Neighbourhood (1914-39)   £18.50
Portrait of Gentleman's Row (Reg Williams)   £9.50
Treasures of Enfield (Editor: Valerie Carter)   £13.50
Six Heritage Walks in the London Borough of Enfield
    (Editor: Monica Smith)   £6.50
Enfield Quiz Book (Betty Smith)   £1.50
Heritage Walk 1 — Forty Hill and Bulls Cross   £1.00
Heritage Walk 2 — Enfield Town   £1.00
Heritage Walk 3 — Edmonton   £ 1.00

The above can be purchased from Waterstone's Bookshop, 26 Church Street, Enfield.

Other retail outlets sell maps, walks leaflets, Christmas cards and postcards. All items are available from The Enfield Society, Jubilee Hall, 2 Parsonage Lane, Enfield, EN2 6QB and a full list can be found on the website: www.enfieldsociety.org.uk.

Index

Abbey Road, Bush Hill Park 32
Advanced Level Certificate 148
AEC Lighting 178
AFS, *see* Auxiliary Fire Service
Agriculture, Ministry of 197
air ambulance 134, 135
air pollution 58-9, 134
Air Raid Precautions 11, 14, 21, 22, 43
    90, 113, 122, 167
air-raid shelters 13
air raids 11, 14, 90, 94, 138
Albany School, Enfield Wash 59
Albu, Austen MP 46, 47, 54, 77
Alcazar Cinema, Edmonton 28, 89, 90
Alexandra, Princess 144, 146
All Saints Church, Edmonton 82
Alma Road School, Ponders End 52
Alpha Road, Edmonton 82
Ambrose Fleming Technical Grammar
    School 151, 193
ambulance stations 15
Anderson shelters 13, 14-15, 28
Angel Centre, Edmonton 85
Angel House tower block, Edmonton
    65-7, 68, 82
Angel Road, Edmonton 25, 175
anti-aircraft guns 17, 18
anti-tank defences 21, 110
Arnos Grove
    Library and Swimming Pool 96, 100
    Underground Station 28, 113
ARP, *see* Air Raid Precautions
athletics 105
Atlas Lighting 176
Attlee, Prime Minister Clement 36, 45
ATS, *see* Auxiliary Territorial Service
Attenborough, Richard 94
automated teller machine, World's first
    76
Auxiliary Fire Service 14

Auxiliary Territorial Service 17, 50, 69
Avery, David 87
Aylward, Gladys 92

Balcon, Sir Michael 91
Barclays Bank, Enfild 76
barrage balloons 17
Barrowell Green, Winchmore Hill 40. 41
    Swimming Baths 15, 99
Bart, Lionel 96
Battle of Britain 27-8
Baxter, Sir Beverley, MP 36, 54, 77, 79
BBC 15, 92, 100
Beatles, The 72
Beaverbrook, Lord 170
Beeching Report 112
Bell Equipment factory 160
Bell Lane, Enfield Highway 31
Bell public house, Southgate 203
Belling & Co Ltd, Southbury Road 159,
    160, 176, 178
Belling & Lee Ltd, Great Cambridge
    Road 153, 157, 159
Berlin airlift 52
Berry, Sir Anthony, MP 72, 75, 76, 77,
    152
Birch, Dr Allan 122
Beveridge Report 36
blackout, wartime 17, 113
Blitz, London 20, 113, 122, 124, 137
Bloomfield, Mrs P. 124
bomb damage, wartime 11, 26-8, 31, 33,
    90, 113, 124, 126, 140, 157, 159, 160,
    172
Bomb Disposal Unit 140
Boundary Commission 44
Bounds Green Underground Station 28,
    113
Bowes Park Methodist Church 37, 72
Braintree, Essex 20, 137, 138

Bray, Christopher 76
Bren gun 167, 168, 169
brickmaking 155, 157
Brigadier Hill, Enfield 199
Brimsdown
    Power Station 120, 153, 157
    Signal Box 110
British Legion 100
British Medical Association 130
British Nationality Act 46
British Oxygen Co, Edmonton 33, 175-7
British Railways, Eastern Region 110
British Restaurants 27
British Sangamo Co 157
British Transport Commission 120, 160
Broomfield House and Park, Palmers
    Green 15, 16, 33, 61, 122
Broughton, Eric, architect 58, 82
Broxbourne, Hertfordshire 168
bullpup rifle 171
Bulls Cross Farm 100
Bullsmoor Lane, Enfield 31
Bush Hill Park 25, 28, 32, 33, 68, 98, 203
    Railway Station 85
Butler, Rab, MP 140 140
Bycullah Estate 41
Bycullah Road, Enfield 22, 68

Campaign for Nuclear Disarmament 53
Canonbury Cottages, Enfield 188
Capel Manor 67, 148, 150
capital punishment 69
Capitol Cinema, Winchmore Hill 91
car parks 120
Cardinal Allen School 151
Carpenter Gardens, Winchmore Hill 33
Carter , Valerie 179
Carterhatch School, Enfield 146
Carterhatch Lane, Enfield 157
Cartland, Barbara 72
Castle, Barbara, MP 120
Cattlegate Road, Enfield 199
Cecil Road, Enfield 120, 183, 184
censorship 15, 72
Chapel Street, Enfield 14
Chamberlain, Prime Minister Neville 14
Chace Boys School, Enfield 140, 143,
    151, 152
Chase Farm Hospital 15, 122, 123, 129,
    180
Chace Girls School, Enfield 151
Chase Green, Enfield 177

Chase Road, Southgate 68, 82, 203
Chase Side, Enfield 199
Chase Side School, Enfield 137
Chaseside Engineering Co Ltd, Great
    Cambridge Road 159
Cheshunt, Hertfordshire 41, 79
Chesterfield Road School 30, 31
child allowance 43
Christ Church, Enfield 82, 199
Christ Church, Southgate 76
church attendance 92
Church Hill, Winchmore Hill 87
Church House, Southgate 92, 96
Church Lane, Enfield 185
Church Street Edmonton 202
Church Street, Enfield 55
Churchbury Railway Station, *see*
    Southbury Railway Station
Churchill, Winston, Prime Minister 15-
    16, 17, 36, 37, 77, 140, 170, 173
Churchill, Mary, *see* Soames, Lady
cinemas 15, 22, 27, 28, 90-2
City and Guilds exams 150
Civic Amenities Act 87, 199
Civic Trust Award 82, 201
Civil Defence 23, 33, 42
Clacton-on-Sea, Essex 18, 137
Clapton-Cheshunt railway line 112
Clark, Kenneth 100
Clay Hill 21, 195, 197, 202
Clean Air Act 59, 175
Clements, John 94
closed shop policy 44, 82
clothes 46, 47, 70, 72
    rationing 30
clothing coupons 29, 30, 47
CND, *see* Campaign for Nuclear
    Disarmament
Cock, The, Palmers Green 121
Cockfosters 59, 114, 145
    Underground Station 28, 111, 113,
    114
Cockfosters, HMS, Hadley Wood 22
Cold War 37, 52, 171
Collegiate School, Winchmore Hill 146
Commonwealth Immigration Act 76
comprehensive education 151
Congregational Church, Ponders End 28
conscientious objectors 20
conscription, military 20
conservation areas 84, 85, 86, 87, 199,
    200, 202

Coopers Lane Road, Hertfordshire 182, 191, 193
Cornish Brickworks, Hoe Lane 155
Coronation 59-61, 91
Cosmocord 157
Cosmos Manufacturing Co Ltd, Brimsdown 159
Council housing 40, 41
Coward, Noel 90, 91, 96
Crews Hill Railway Station 112
cricket 97, 103
Crown & Horseshoes public house, Enfield 198, 201
Crown Brick Works, Southbury Road 157
Crown Tavern 203
Cuckoo Hall Estate, Edmonton 13, 39, 41, 145

D-Day invasion 33, 140
'Dad's Army', see Home Guard
Dalling, Graham 54
dancing 72, 92
Darby and Joan clubs 100
Davies, Ernest, MP 36, 54
De Bohun Health Clinic, Southgate 131
Delhi Road, Enfield 39
Denny, Douglas 150
devaluation of the pound 77
Devon House Winchmore Hill Green 200
diesel locomotives 107, 110
'Dig for Victory' 24, 25, 190
Domestic Help 131
drugs, illegal 76
Durants Road, Ponders End 28
Durbin, Evan, MP 36, 41, 46

Ealing Studios 91
Eastern Gas Board 54
Eastfield Road, Enfield 27
Edison Swan Electric Light Co Ltd 46, 153, 159, 160, 175, 178
Edmonton 20, 33, 36, 38, 42, 43, 46, 51, 52, 54, 77, 79, 82, 85, 87, 114, 120, 122, 135, 136, 138, 143, 157, 203
    Council 59, 81, 82, 87, 100
    Education Officer 150
    Green 49, 85
    Lower Level Railway Station 106
    Railway Junction 109
    Town Hall 41, 59

Edmonton County School 20, 138, 143, 151
Edmonton History Association 87
Edmonton Hundred Historical Society 87, 202
education 69, 78, 136ff
Education Act 140
Education, Minister of 140, 150, 152
Eldon School, Edmonton 20
electrical appliances 45-6, 55, 160, 175-6
Eleven Plus exam 140
Elizabeth, Princess 45, 50
Elizabeth II, Queen 56, 58, 59
Elizabeth, Queen Mother 149, 152
Elsyng Palace 63
Empire Cinema, Edmonton 91
Empire's Best coaches 120
Enfield
    Borough Charter 57, 58
    Borough Council 181, 183, 191, 193, 197, 201, 202
    Civic Centre, 78, 79, 80, 82, 183
    East 44, 53, 77, 82, 136
    Education Committee 76
    Highway 41
    Lock 105, 114, 160, 166, 170, 172
    Market Place 184
    Playing Fields 17, 98, 105
    Police Station 59
    Public Offices, Gentleman's Row 56, 58
    Swimming Pool 105
    Town 20, 48, 51, 84, 87, 115, 118, 120, 121, 183, 184, 187, 188, 199
    Town Railway Station 109, 112, 197
    Urban District Council 41, 43, 56, 57, 58, 62, 82, 179, 204
    Wash 53
    West 44, 53, 77, 87
    West Underground Staion 28, 113
Enfield & District Manufacturers' Association 175
Enfield Archaeological Society 63
Enfield Cables Ltd 159
'Enfield Can Do It' exhibition 175
Enfield Central School 151
Enfield Chase 197
    Railway Station 112
Enfield Collegiate School 52, 145, 146
Enfield Co-operative Women's Guild 77
Enfield County School 137, 138, 139, 140, 151, 204

Enfield Football Club 97, 100
Enfield Grammar School 58, 77, 78, 121, 151, 152, 183, 199
Enfield Grammar School Old Boys Association 183
Enfield Preservation Society 78, 87, 179ff
Enfield Technical College 77, 150
EPS, see Enfield Preservation Soviety
evacuation, wartime 15, 18, 19-20, 113, 136-7
Evans and Davies, Department Store, Palmers Green 15, 104
Eversley School, Winchmore Hill 145
Express Motor & Body Works Ltd, Great Cambridge Road 158

Fairfield Road, Edmonton 31
family planning clinics 134
Famine Relief Committee 37
fashion, see clothes
Federation of Enfield Ratepayers and Residents Associations 57, 77, 183, 202
Ferguson's Radio Corporation Ltd 160, 161
FERRA, see Federation of Enfield Ratepayers and Residents Associations
Festival of Britain 55
Finsbury Park Railway Station 114
Fir Tree House, Enfield 78
Fire Service 12, 14, 43
Firs Farm Playing Fields 17
Firs Hall, Winchmore Hill 92, 203
Florida Cinema, Enfield 90
food 25, 27, 38, 44, 47, 87, 130, 157
    rationing 25, 37, 47, 130
Food, Ministry of 27, 38, 90
Food Office 38
football 97, 100
Football Association Amateur Cup 100
footpaths 190-1, 199
Fo re Street, Edmonton 31, 44, 68, 72
Forest Road, Edmonton 77
Forty Hall 50, 56, 57, 62, 63, 67, 85, 200, 203
Forty Hill 67, 85, 87, 114, 197, 199, 200
    Railway Station, see Turkey Street Railway Station
Forty Hill and Bulls Cross Study Group 201
Forty Hill Primary School 142

Fox Lane, Palmers Green 142, 145
    Bridge 33
fuel supplies 54, 68
furniture 47
Fry, Helen 30

gardens and allotments 25, 100
gasmasks 12
General Certificate of Education 148
Genotin Road, Enfield 199
Gentleman's Row, Enfield 56, 58, 65, 67, 180, 201
George VI, King 50, 58, 169
George Ewer's Grey Green Coaches 120
Gilpin Crescent, Edmonton 40
Goat public house, Forty Hill 114
golf 98, 105
Gordon Hill, Enfield 13, 33, 195
    Railway Station 107, 110, 112
Gough Park 188, 189
Gough Park Cottage, Clay Hill 197
Gowers, Robert 188
GPO Film Unit 91
Grange Park 145
    Railway Station 112
Grenada Cinema, Edmonton 91
Great Cambridge Road 31, 121, 153
Greater London Council 69, 79, 197
green belt 41, 77, 195
Green Lanes, Palmers Green 27, 28
Greenline buses 120
Greenwood, Anthony, MP 82, 152, 187
Gresswell, Don 182, 183, 188, 193, 199
Grovelands Hospital, Southgate 15, 127, 129
Groves, Godfrey 181, 201

Hackney, Mayor of 105
Hadley Wood 22
    Railway Station 112
    railway tunnel 108, 112
Hannah, John 197
Harlow New Town exhibition 41
Harvey, Miss K., Enfield Mayor 78, 80, 204
Healey, Maurice 150
health 122ff
Health, Ministry of 122
Hedge Lane 21
Hertford East and North railway lines, 112
Hertford Road, Edmonton 134

Higgins, Peter 58
High View Gardens, New Southgate 42
Higher School Certificate exams 138,
    148
Highlands Hospital 15, 126, 127
Hill House, Winchmore Hill 87
Hilly Fields 44, 92
Hippies 72
Hippodrome Cinema, Edmonton 91
hire purchase 55
Hispano cannon 171
historic buildings, demolition 62, 68, 73,
    83, 84, 87
Hodge, Dr J. 77
Hodson, Mrs 180
Hoe Lane, Enfield 155
holidays 46, 68, 87, 105
Holly Hill Farm, Enfield 103, 193
Holly Walk, Enfield 77, 121, 183, 186
Holtwhites Hill, Enfield 52
Holy Family School 151
Home Guard 21, 42, 43, 113, 167
Home Help 131
homosexuality 69, 72
Hoppers Road, Winchmore Hill 21
Hornsey, Borough of 79
Horticulture 157
hospitals 122ff
Houndsfield School, Edmonton 15, 77,
    136, 140, 145
housing 38, 41, 52, 68, 77, 82
Housing, Minister of 186-7

identity cards 20
immigration 52, 76, 92, 203
industry 33,153ff
Information, Ministry of 91
Intimate Theatre 15, 92-6
Islington Cemetery, Trent Park 45
Islington Council 45

Jarvis, Rupert 199
Jay, Mrs, Enfield UDC Chairman 47, 48
Jephcott, Christopher 182, 187, 188
Johnson Matthey & Co Ltd 160, 176
Joyce, Tom 41

Kaye, E. & E., Ponders End 157
Keble Preparatory School, Winchmore
    Hill, 138
King George Playing Fields, Enfield 31
Korean War 52, 170

Lacey Hall, Palmers Green 72
Lamb Institute, Edmonton 90
Land Army 19, 20, 25
Lane, Carinthia Arbuthnot 180, 181, 187
Lane, Dame Elizabeth 204
Lane, Tony 180, 182
Latymer Foundation 150
Latymer School, The, Edmonton 20,
    136, 137, 138, 149, 150, 151
Lavender Hill, Enfield 33, 82, 136, 195
Lea, River 102, 105, 119, 120, 153
Lea Valley 110
    armaments factories 53, 69
    market gardens 25, 33, 156
Lee Enfield rifle 172
Leigh, Vivien 93
leisure 88ff
Lend Lease agreement 37
libraries 95, 100
Library Green, Enfield 11, 179
listed buildings 67
Little Amwell, Hertfordshire 68
Little Park, Gentleman's Row, Enfield
    87, 181
Little Pipers, Clay Hill 195, 197
Local Defence Volunteers, *see* Home
    Guard
local government reorganisation 78-9
London and Middlesex Archaeological
    Society 199
London
    bombing 28
    County Council 69
    Lord Mayor of 57
    Museum of 186
    Transport 114, 119
    Underground 28, 110, 112-13
London Borough of Enfield 78, 79, 82,
    121, 135, 150, 151, 193, 204
    coat-of-arms 78, 79
London Country Buses 119
London Hospital 126
London North Eastern Railway 110
London Passenger Transport Board 113,
    114, 119
London Philharmonic Orchestra 96
London Road, Enfield 28
    Roman Catholic Church 28, 92

Mackie, John, MP 77, 82, 191
Macleod, Iain, MP 53-4, 69, 77, 87, 152
Macmillan, Harold, MP 65, 68

McWhirter, Ross 82
Maidens Bridge 202
manufacturing 153ff
Mapleton Road, Enfield Highway 32, 33
Margaret, Princess 132, 134, 146, 148
Marr, Andrew 51
Marshall Aid 37
Matriculation exams 138
Meals on Wheels 42, 81
Metal Box Co 33
Metro Cammell railway trains 113, 114
Middlesex County Council 45, 78-9, 132, 135, 150, 183
Middlesex Polytechnic 150
Minchenden Lower School, Southgate 142, 145
Minchenden School, Southgate 77, 133, 137-8, 147, 150, 151
Moral Welfare Association 76
Morrison shelters 28
motor buses 114, 115, 116, 117, 118, 119, 203
motor cars 68, 120-1, 203
motor scooters 71, 72
Mountbatten, Lt Philip 45
Mullard Space Science Laboratory 77
Myddelton Avenue, Enfield 188
Myddelton House, Bulls Cross 62, 63, 67

Nairn, Ian 186
Napley, David 184
National Health Service 36, 43, 129, 120, 130-2, 134, 204
National Service 42, 69, 172
nationalisation 43
Nazeing 191
New Coronation Cinema, New Southgate 91
New River 28, 78, 131, 183, 192
New Southgate 33, 41, 72, 75, 82, 112, 157, 160, 161, 163
Nightingale Road, Edmonton 52
North Circular Road 121, 153
North Middlesex Hospital, Edmonton 15, 31, 124-6, 130, 132, 133, 135
Northern Hospital, Winchmore Hill 126
Northern Regional Centre 126, 129
Northmet 38
Novello, Ivor 94

Oakwood 52, 72, 114
    Park 19

Underground Station 28, 113
Oakwood Secondary Modern School 141, 151
Odeon Cinema, Southgate 90, 91
Old Bakery, Forty Hill 87, 197, 199
Old Park Avenue, Enfield 184
Old Southgate 41
Old Vestry House, Enfield 180
Olivier, Laurence 91
Olympic Games 46, 58, 165
O'Neill, Eugene 94
Ordnance Road, Enfield Lock 31, 82
Ordinary Level Certificate 148
Orwell, George 69
Osborne, John 96

Palmadium Cinema, Palmers Green 91
Palmer, William 184, 188
Palmers Green 27, 28, 49, 52, 61, 104, 105, 114, 148
    Railway Station 33, 112
Palmers Green Baptist Church
Palmers Green High School 138, 146
Pam, David 11
Paulin Ground, Winchmore Hill 105
Pearsons store 46
Peartree Road, Enfield 28
Perry, Frances 150
Peto Scott Electrical Instruments Ltd, Great Cambridge Road 159
petrol
    coupons 17
    rationing 25, 68, 119
Pevensey Avenue, New Southgate 31
Piccadilly Underground Line 112-13, 114
Picketts Lock, Edmonton 105
Pinter, Harold 96
Pioneer Corps 28
Plaza Cinema, Ponders End 90
Ponders End 26, 82, 120, 190
    High Road 28
    Gas Works 154, 157
    Library 95, 100
    Recreation Ground 92
    Railway Station 21, 106, 110
    Sewage Works 28
Ponders End Flour Mills 59, 157, 158, 202
Ponders End Garage 59, 114
Ponders End Girls School 151
pop music 72
population 51

elderly 82
Portcullis House, Enfield 79
Potter, Donald 182, 183
Potters Bar, Hertfordshire 41, 79, 82
Powys Lane, Southgate 84, 87
'prefab' bungalows 38, 39, 41
Premier Cinema, Enfield 91
Priestley, J. B. 69
Princes Dance Hall, Palmers Green 28, 92
prisoners of war 29, 30-1, 33, 45, 145, 156
Profumo Affair 76
Progressive Synagogue, Southgate 92
protests 85
Pymmes House and Park, Edmonton 15, 16, 33, 34, 44, 92, 96

Queen's Award for Industry 176
Queens Cinema, Palmers Green 91
Queen's Medal for Poetry 105
Queensway, Ponders End 157

Race Relations Act 52, 76, 85
radio 15, 92
railway
    electrification 109, 110, 112
    stations 21, 106ff
Rainbird, Kenneth 130
Ramblers' Association 199
Rattigan, Terence 92
ration books 23, 38
rationing, *see* clothes, food and petrol rationing
Raynham Road School, Edmonton 137
Rays Road, Edmonton 85
Red Cross 43, 53, 59
Rees, Rev Ebenezer 181, 197, 199
refugees, wartime 23
Regal Cinema, Edmonton, 72, 88, 90, 91, 96
Representation of the People Act 44
resale price maintenance 73
Reservoir Road, Southgate 36
Rialto Cinema, Enfield 91
Ridge Avenue Library 95, 100
Ridgeway, The, Enfield 68, 179, 194, 197, 203
Ridgeway Farm, 179
ring road, Enfield 121, 183, 184, 185, 186
Ripaults Ltd, Southbury Road 158, 160, 175
Ritz Cinema, New Southgate 91

road accidents, 134
road safety campaigns 47, 76, 121
roads 77, 121
Robson, Dame Flora 148
rock 'n' roll 70, 72
Rockers 72
Rolling Stones, The 72
Roman Catholic Church, London Road, Enfield 28, 92
Rose & Crown, Clay Hill 21, 64, 67
Routemaster buses 114, 116,118
Rowantree School 151
Royal Gunpowder Factory, Waltham Abbey 167
Royal Northern Hospital 129
Royal Small Arms Factory, Enfield Lock 21, 28, 120, 160, 166-75
Royal Wedding 45
Royalty Dance Hall, Winchmore Hill 92
Ruberoid Co Ltd 160
Ruth Winston House, Palmers Green, 82

St Andrew's Church and Vicarage, Enfield 58, 59, 64, 67, 121, 183, 184, 185, 186
St Angela's Convent School 138, 151
St Faith's Cottage, Brigadier Hill 196, 197
St Ignatius School 151
St John's Ambulance Brigade 43, 53, 59, 126
St Johns Church, Palmers Green 82
St Joseph's Home, Holtwhites Hill, Enfield 52
St Mary Magdalene Vicarage, Enfield 75, 76
St Mary the Virgin Church, Edmonton 46
St Matthews Church, Ponders End 28
St Michael's Hospital , Enfield 128, 129, 133, 197
St Monica's Church Hall, Green Lanes 92, 96
St Paul's C of E Primary School, Winchmore Hill 144, 146
St Paul's Institute, Winchmore Hill 92
St Peter and St Paul Church 31
Salisbury House, Edmonton 94, 100
Salute the Soldier campaign 138
Sangamo Weston Ltd 160
Sarnesfield Road, Enfield 159

Saracens Rugby Club, Southgate 100
Save Enfield Action Committee 183, 184,
    186, 187
Savoy Cinema, Enfield 22, 90, 91
schools 136ff
School Certificate exams 138, 148
Seven Sisters Underground Station 114
Shakespeare Cottages, Southgate 62
Sharp , Dame Evelyn 203
Sharp, Miss F. 138
Sharp, Miss M. C. 143
Shepherd, Major 170
Shindy Boutique, Enfield 70
shopping 104, 105
Silver End, Essex, 20
Silver Street, Edmonton 116
Silver Street, Enfield 82, 129, 130, 196,
    199
Silver Street School, Edmonton 137
Skilton, Alan 186
Slades Hill, Enfield 17, 18, 124
slum clearance 40
Smith, Stevie 105, 148
Smithfield Meat Market, London 25, 27,
    44
smog, *see* air pollution
Soames, Lady 17, 69
South Lodge Hospital 129
South Street, Ponders End 28
Southbury Railway Station 110, 112, 194,
    197
Southbury Road 22, 28, 159, 160
Southgate 14, 20, 27, 33, 36, 38, 41, 44,
    51, 54, 58, 59, 68, 79, 82, 84, 114, 122,
    129, 132, 133, 137, 143
    Council 11, 41, 59
    Green 59, 67, 73, 86, 87, 200, 202
    Library 100
    Swimming Pool 99, 105
    Underground Station 28, 110, 113
    Village Hall 62
Southgate Civic Society 73, 74, 87, 199,
    202
Southgate College 147, 150
Southgate County School 145, 151
Southgate Harriers 46, 58
Southgate Isolation Hospital 132
Spears, J. W., & Sons Ltd, Brimsdown 92,
    159
Splinternet adhesive fabric 33
sport 100, 103-4
Stadium Ltd, Ponders End 157

Standard Fuse Company, Ponders End
    157
Standard Telephones and Cables, New
    Southgate 160, 161-6
STC New Southgate Radio Engineering
    Society 165
Sten gun 170, 173
strikes 68, 119
Suez crisis 68-9, 121
supermarkets 37-8, 55, 96
Suffolk School 151
Sussex Way, Cockfosters 145
swimming pools 99, 105
Sykes, Robert Dugdale 197

tank manufacture 156
Tank Repair Unit 22
Teddy boys 70
television 15, 59, 91, 100, 160, 176
Temple Bar 187
'That Was The Week That Was' 72
Thompson, Colin 156
Thompson's Nursery 156
Tonypandy, Wales 136, 137
Tottenham 72, 79, 135, 138
Tottenham Hale Railway Station 114
tower blocks 41, 42, 66-8, 82, 85, 203
transport 106ff
trade unions 68, 82
tree planting 74, 193, 195, 197
tree preservation orders 67
Trent Park and Estate 29, 30, 45, 148,
    150
Trent Park Teacher Training College 45,
    146, 148, 203
Triangle, The, Palmers Green 49, 121
Tricity Cookers Ltd 160
Trinity County School, Wood Green 138
trolleybuses 114, 115, 116, 118, 203
Turkey Brook, Enfield 82
Turkey Street (formerly Forty Hill)
    Railway Station 112
Turpin, Harold 170, 173
Two Brewers public house, Ponders End
    28

United Flexible Tubing, Scotland Green
    Road, Ponders End 31
Universal Matthey Products 176
University of London School of
    Pharmacy, 62

V1 and V2 rockets 31-3, 126, 140, 163, 165
vandalism 46-7, 68, 85, 87, 96
vegetable growing 156
Vicarage Farm, Enfield 180
Vicars Moor Lane, Winchmore Hill 202
Vickers machine gun 167
Victoria Underground Line 114
Victory in Europe 33, 34
Victory over Japan 34
Victory parades 42-3
Vietnam war 77

wages 55
Walker Ground, Southgate 97
Walker, Patrick Gordon-, MP 152
Walker Primary School, Southgate 143
Waltham Abbey, Essex 167
Waltham Cross, Hertfordshire 118
War Memorial Cottage Hospital, Enfield 128, 129
water transport 119, 120
weather, severe 44, 62, 73, 96, 113, 116
weddings 38
Welfare State 203
Wellington Road, Bush Hill Park 203
Whitaker, Cuthbert 188
White Lodge, Silver Street, Enfield 196, 199

White Lodge Surgery, Enfield 129, 130
Whitewebbs Lane 188
Wilbury Way, Edmonton 126
Willow Road, Enfield 26, 28
Wilson, Harold, Prime Minister, 87
Winchmore Hill 33, 52, 67, 72, 82, 118, 129, 146, 202, 203
  Green 83, 86, 87, 200, 202
  Railway Station 107, 112
  Swimming Pool 105
Winchmore Hill Garage 25
Windmill Hill 159
  Railway Bridge 180
Wings for Victory campaign 138
Winston, Ruth 204
Witham, Essex 20
Wolfenden Committee 69
Wood Green 36, 44, 54
women, employment and rights 45, 72, 156, 158, 159, 204
Women's Voluntary Service 21-2, 42, 53, 62, 81, 85
World War II 11ff, 88, 90, 122ff, 167
Wrights Flour Mill, *see* Ponders End Flour Mills
WVS and WRVS, *see* Women's Voluntary Service

Young Fashionables, Edmonton 72